D0454806

Sales Magic

KERRY L. JOHNSON

Sales Magic

Revolutionary New Techniques That Will Double Your Sales Volume in 21 Days

QUILL
WILLIAM MORROW
New York

Copyright © 1994 by Nightingale-Conant Corporation

All rights reserved. No part of this book may be reproduced or utilized in any form or by any means, electronic or mechanical, including photocopying, recording, or by any information storage or retrieval system, without permission in writing from the Publisher. Inquiries should be addressed to Permissions Department, William Morrow and Company, Inc., 1350 Avenue of the Americas, New York, N.Y. 10019.

It is the policy of William Morrow and Company, Inc., and its imprints and affiliates, recognizing the importance of preserving what has been written, to print the books we publish on acid-free paper, and we exert our best efforts to that end.

LIBRARY OF CONGRESS CATALOGING-IN-PUBLICATION DATA

Johnson, Kerry L.
    Sales magic : revolutionary new techniques that will double your
sales volume in 21 days / Kerry L. Johnson.
        p.   cm.
    ISBN 0-688-14233-8
    1. Selling.   2. Selling—Psychological aspects.   I. Title.
HF5438.25.J6534   1994
658.85—dc20   93-28826
                                                                    CIP

Printed in the United States of America

First Quill Edition

1   2   3   4   5   6   7   8   9   10

To my wife, Merita,
who is a constant source of
support and love

Acknowledgments

I wish to thank Andy Ambraziejus, who significantly contributed to the prose of this book. Thanks also to Jill Schacter, Georgene Cevasco, and Mike Willbond for their unwaivering belief in the message that *Sales Magic* conveys, and for their editorial help. Gratitude also goes to Margo Montgomery for her editing and administrative assistance.

Contents

The Magic of Trust

John Milam, an insurance and financial services salesman from Knoxville, Tennessee, was waiting patiently in the reception area of a manufacturing company. He had an appointment with the company owner, to whom he hoped to sell a million dollars' worth of life insurance and make a fifty-thousand-dollar commission. But his client was thirty minutes late. All John could do was wait.

Finally, John's prospective client appeared, hurriedly making his way to his own office. Seeing John in the reception area, the client walked over to him. His arms were crossed—he was obviously not in the mood to buy. "Uh, John, I . . . I can't see you this morning. I . . . I'm too busy," he told him, trying to brush him off.

John stood up, crossing his own arms. "Would you like to reschedule this?" he asked his client. The client seemed to soften. "How long will this take if I see you right now?" he asked. John smiled. "Ten minutes—unless you ask me any questions."

"Well, if that's all it'll take, I'll talk to you right now, rather than postpone this," the company owner told him, indicating by the look on his face that John shouldn't expect anything more from him. Ten minutes later, however, John emerged from the client's office, having closed the sale.

What was John's secret? What did he say or do in those short but profitable minutes to convince his client to buy his product? What was it about the way John reacted to his client that got him ten minutes of the man's time in the first place?

As you read this book, you will discover that John's secret is both simple and profound. In the late 1970s, after two years of playing professional tennis—and realizing I wasn't about to win Wimbledon—I decided to pursue my two interests, sales and human behavior, working as a stockbroker and studying for a Ph.D. in psychology. My studies led me to an exciting new area of research being done at the University of California at Santa Cruz. Called NeuroLinguistic Programming (NLP), this field of psychology examines the different ways people think and communicate with one another. It also isolates ways to model excellence.

The founders of NLP, Richard Bandler and John Grinder, studied the working methods of therapists who were very successful with their clients. Although all the therapists worked differently, there was one thing they had in common: They were very good at gaining their clients' trust. If trust is present in the relationship between client and therapist, the work of therapy succeeds. Trust motivates. Trust helps a client work through problems more completely.

Until recently, no one seemed to know exactly why trust developed in some therapeutic relationships and not in others. Bandler and Grinder gave us a very interesting answer to that question: *We all have different ideas of reality—ways in which we perceive the world—and we can only really trust people who look at the world the way we do.* If we feel understood, we give people our trust and open up to them more easily.

The more I studied the research, the more I began to wonder whether it could be applied to the sales situation as well. After all, what is sales but making money through communication? Were the million-dollar sales producers—those lucky few men and women who made over a million dollars in commissions every year—able to communicate trust to their clients in some magical, unconscious way? If the average salesperson studied their methods, could he or she do everything the supersellers could?

In 1980, I formed my own company, International Productivity Systems, and began studying these supersellers in earnest. What they did really seemed magical: getting their clients to buy without appearing to try very hard. But when I asked them how they did it, they had no idea, shrugging their shoulders and saying it was the result of twenty or thirty years of sales experience. Then I began to apply the dynamics uncovered by NLP as I watched how they dealt with their clients. The magic became commonplace, and I could see clearly what was happening and why. It is this magic I want to share with you in my book.

If you master the techniques described on the following pages, I guarantee you will gain three things:

1. You are going to discover more about your prospective clients in five minutes than you previously could in two weeks.

2. You will learn to predict how your clients will buy.

3. You will learn how to let your clients sell to themselves.

Sales Magic presents an entirely new system of selling, based on trust. The first section will teach you to become a detective of human behavior. You will learn that people have different modes of thinking and how those modes affect their decisions to buy. You will learn what your clients really mean when they talk with you, and how you can use this information to communicate with them more effectively. And you will learn how to gain their trust by presenting your product in those modes.

In the second section, you will learn specific selling techniques that you can apply in all situations. You will learn how to reinforce the trust you have gained and communicate with your clients on deeper, ever more subtle, levels. Using both verbal and physical techniques, you will learn how to pace your sales meetings. And using your knowledge of buying behavior, you will be able to guide your clients to make decisions they otherwise might be afraid to make.

I now make my living writing books on sales and management psychology and giving seminars and presentations to companies all over the world. Since that first year as a stockbroker when I received 149 rejections out of every 150 calls, I have increased my earnings significantly by mastering the techniques based on NLP principles.

I think what I've learned can benefit you in the same way. Selling can be magic, but a magic based on understanding specific buying patterns and rules of sales psychology. By mastering the skills presented in this book, you will be able to build up your business as well. As a matter of fact, I guarantee that you will double your sales within the first year. I think it's a magic anyone who sells can appreciate.

Note: In sales literature, a prospective client is technically referred to as a prospect. However, I find that term rather cold and dehumanizing. Throughout the book, I have used *customer* and *client* wherever I could, both of which better express the human element of the selling process.

PART I

THE PSYCHOLOGY OF BUYING AND SELLING

People buy trust first, products second.

CHAPTER ONE

How People Buy: Seeing Your Client Through Your Client's Eyes

"If you can see John Smith through John Smith's eyes, you will sell John Smith what John Smith buys."

This is a motto of sorts at International Productivity Systems, Inc., the company I founded in 1980 to study the country's top salespeople. We have learned that selling to people the way they want to buy is the single most important element of every superseller's repertoire. No matter what their style, service, or product, no matter whether the price or fee is large or small, the most effective salespeople seem to have an uncanny ability to size up their prospective clients or customers accurately. They are able to pick up behavioral cues that reveal how their prospective purchasers would make buying decisions. They know what their clients would say. They are able to predict how their customers make decisions. In short, they seem to know their clients and customers almost as well as they know themselves.

It wasn't too long ago that sales was seen as an adversarial relationship. On the receiving end of the sales pitch, a client was someone on guard, afraid of being manipulated into buying something he or she didn't want. The salesperson was taught to do just that—to counter this hostility by outmaneuvering customers with expert sales pitches and manipulation. The profession had such a bad reputation that salespeople were reluctant to admit who they actually were.

This attitude has made a 180-degree about-face during the last decade or so. Sales professionals have begun to acknowledge the importance of the client's input to the sales process. Terms such as *relationship selling*, *personalized selling*, and *insightful selling* have been thrown around in articles and speeches. A few years ago, in a piece he'd written for the *Harvard Business Review*, best-selling author Harvey Mackay wrote that at his company, Mackay Envelope, salespeople had to have a sixty-six-point dossier on each prospective customer. "The point here is that people don't truly care how much you know until they know how much you care," wrote Mr. Mackay. I agree with him. No matter how good your product is, how articulate you are, or how good a deal you are offering, if you forget that there is a human being on the other side of the desk, you are losing the point of what sales is all about.

We at International Productivity Systems have taken the concept of knowing your client one step further. We have discovered that it is not so much what or how much you know about your customers that is important, but the trust you gain from showing them that you are in their corner. People buy trust first, products second. Trust can overcome a higher price or even lackluster servicing of your product. If clients sense that you are with them and not trying to manipulate them, they will be more willing to listen, to learn what your product or service can do for them. Trust is what will keep them interested and what will get them to spend their money.

In experiment after experiment, researchers have reported that trust is crucial in successful selling. If trust is present, clients are more receptive to suggestions, give more time to a salesperson, and schedule appointments earlier in the day. They are also more likely to open up, discuss needs and buying habits, and inform salespeople about future plans. If the risk is high and the dollar amount of a potential deal considerable, trust is even more crucial to a sale.

The new interest in trust has spawned some rather interesting rituals. At a Jacksonville, Florida, auto dealership, for example, the general manager climbs up a ladder, pauses, counts to two, and then steps backward, falling into the arms of his coworkers. Called a trust fall, it's not a New Age touchy-feely session, but a real attempt to instill the concept into every salesperson. Trust seminars are everywhere.

But what is trust? How is it formed between a client and a salesperson? How do the supersellers get their clients to trust them so thoroughly?

I have been teaching business people that they don't do it by being smarter or more manipulative. They do it because they have what I call unconscious competence.

The Power of the Unconscious

Unconscious competence is communicating with clients at an unconscious level. To illustrate just how powerful the unconscious mind really is, I want to describe an experiment from my graduate-school days in psychology.

As part of my thesis, I rode around on Continental Airlines with several classmates, finding out what people liked and didn't like about the airline. As part of our survey, we would ask people to give an overall score for the service, or the food, or anything else included in the price. For example, we would ask people how they liked the mugs their coffee was served in. The subject would give an overall rating from one to ten. For the purposes of this example, let's say someone gives the mugs a rating of seven.

We would then divide the mug into different components: its size, its color, the shape of the handle, its weight, how it feels. We would get ratings on each component. What we found when we averaged out the scores on the individual components was that they were the same as the overall score. The scores of the person who had given the mug an overall rating of seven, for example, averaged out to seven. If someone had given the mugs an overall score of five, their scores for the different components would average out to five.

This happened over and over again, to a statistically significant degree. Even though our subjects didn't know what we were after, they kept giving an overall score that later turned out to be a composite of the marks for the individual components.

We really don't appreciate how much information is constantly being processed by our unconscious minds, and how quickly it all happens. In the above experiment, we could say that our subjects were guessing at an overall number. Yet, the guessing turned out to be much more exact than merely picking out a number at random. There was quite a bit of calculation involved.

In some ways, I think the supersellers are like these subjects. John Savage, for example, is a financial planner who has earned millions of dollars in commissions. I've heard John speak at sales training seminars, and he lists such principles as working hard, being focused, having clear goals as the ingredients of success. I've heard Jim Rohn, known as the father of motivational speakers, say something similar, then look around at his audience and wonder, "I recognize some of you from before. Why are you here?"

People return because the tried-and-true techniques work a little, but not enough. These supersellers don't seem to have an appreciation for the unconscious ways they are able to build trust and make sales. They don't see the power of their own unconscious competence. But it exists. All you have to do is learn to recognize how it comes out when you interact with your clients.

Mental Maps and Representational Systems

Richard Bandler and John Grinder, the founders of what is now known as NeuroLinguistic Programming (NLP), began their work at the University of California at Santa Cruz in the 1970s. Bandler, a mathematician, and Grinder, a linguist, were both interested in issues of psychotherapy. They began studying the working methods of successful therapists, hoping to provide useful insights for all therapists to follow.

In doing their research, Bandler and Grinder discovered that people have three basic methods of perceiving the world around them:

- Visual
- Auditory
- Kinesthetic

Those people who are visuals *see* the world, the auditories *hear* it, the kinesthetics *feel* it. These three representational systems, or mental maps, are ways of organizing all the stimuli that we receive at any given moment. They help us to understand the world and to relate to it. With these mental maps as guides, we make decisions on how to respond to whatever is going on around us.

The use of mental maps is unconscious. A person doesn't choose which map he or she will use with which to communicate. For that very reason, if you know how to "read" someone's mental map, you have a very powerful tool to use in understanding how someone's mind works. The successful therapists were able to pick up on the mental maps their clients were using and produce results, because they could literally understand how clients were thinking and use that information during psychotherapy.

The same was true for the supersellers we studied. While they were going about their traditional jobs and pitching their products, they were also communicating to their clients the way their clients were communicating to them. The more they did it, the more successful they were.

Like any model of human behavior, the visual/auditory/kinesthetic system makes things appear neater than they really are. No one thinks completely in one mode to the exclusion of the other two. Our minds are constantly at work, processing infinite numbers of stimuli at any given moment. A person switches from one mode to another and back again, depending on a hundred different factors. The important point is to think of mental maps as *preferred* modes of thinking; what a person is most comfortable with; what seems like the most natural way of understanding the world. It is the mode people use when they are most relaxed or unguarded, and it is the mode that produces the strongest reaction when communicated back to a person.

The Visuals

Dan Fouts, former quarterback of the San Diego Chargers football team and an honored member of the Football Hall of Fame, developed a very successful throwing technique called a timing pass. Here's how it worked: His wide receiver went out for a pass. Fouts threw the ball while his receiver was still running away from him, so that when he turned around, the football was already there, hitting him on the numbers.

This pass gave linebackers fits—they found the pass very hard to intercept. Normally, the linebacker tries to look at the receiver's eyes before he tries to intercept a pass. This gives him a clue when and where the ball has been thrown. If the receiver doesn't turn around and wait, the linebacker never knows the ball has been thrown, and can't make the interception.

One reporter, noticing this effective passing technique, walked up to Fouts and said, "Mr. Fouts, you throw the most precise timing pass in the league. How do you do it? What do you think about? What goes through your mind before you throw those bullets?" Dan Fouts said simply, "I go back in the pocket to pass. As I'm waiting for the wide receiver, I see the pass pattern in my head. I see the receiver going down and out, post pattern, around to the side, and then an X in the middle of my mental playing field. I throw the ball to the X that I see in my mind. If the receiver is there, he catches it. If he's not there, nobody catches it.''

Notice the word that Fouts used so often in his response. He *saw* the pass pattern in his head. He *saw* the receiver going down and out. He threw the ball to the X that he *saw* in his mind.

Fouts is a visual: someone who thinks by making pictures in his mind. He understood what was required to make the pass because of what he saw. The images he constructed for himself guided his decisions throughout the entire process. If he hadn't been able to visualize his "mental playing field," he wouldn't have been able to throw the pass accurately.

Bandler and Grinder estimate that about 35 percent of us are visuals. Such people are able to understand something much better if they see it. Their minds turn everything you say into pictures. If you discuss your ideas in visual terms, they smile. Their eyes glow; they understand, they comprehend. They are comfortable with you.

Think of visuals as having minds that work like View-Masters, those periscopelike contraptions with circular slides that we all played with as kids. When you put the View-Master up to your face and pushed the lever, you saw colorful, three-dimensional photographs that made what you were looking at come alive. This is how a visual thinks. When you start talking, he starts clicking the View-Master, understanding your words by comparing them to pictures associated with those words. He is accessing images the entire time you are speaking to him.

Visuals have great visual memories. They can describe how things looked in minute detail. They remember colors, shapes, and forms. They also think in images when fantasizing about the future.

How can you tell that a person is thinking visually? The words and phrases someone uses—what we call *predicates*—are your first clue. Visuals say things like *show:* "Can you show it to me?" *Bright:* "That's a pretty bright idea." *Picture:* "I can picture that." *Clear:* "It's pretty clear to me." *Looks:* "Looks good." Dan Fouts used the word *see* constantly.

Appearance is important for visually oriented people. This was emphasized to me a few years ago by a seemingly trivial incident. I spoke at a sales conference, and during the speech happened to be wearing a suit coat with flaps over the pockets. I hadn't noticed that the flap on one side was tucked inside the pocket, while the other flap was on the outside.

After completing my speech, I went to the back of the room to mingle with the conference participants. One woman came up to me and said, "Kerry, I thought it was a wonderful speech, but I was really distracted for the first fifteen minutes of your talk, because I couldn't take my eyes off that flap on your jacket. I had trouble paying attention to anything you were saying."

Honestly! Not being visually oriented myself, I think of such a reaction as silly. But the point is, there are people who are bothered by any kind of dissymmetry in how you dress, how your office might look, or anything else they notice about you or your environment. Think about it. That is why "dressing for success" is so important in sales—or for that matter, any other profession in which you are presenting something to a client. There are many people who will become distracted from your sales pitch if something is visually off. They want it all to look good, and if it doesn't, you will have a harder time getting their attention.

Eye Movement in the Visual Mode

The second important clue to someone's mental map has to do with eye movement. Bandler and Grinder did videotape studies and found a relationship between the way people think and the way they move their eyes. Watching someone's eye movements as you listen to what they say will give you a very strong indication of what mode they are thinking in.

People who are thinking visually will typically do three things with their eyes:

One, they will look directly up and to the right. This occurs when they are creating images—that is, thinking about the future ("I wonder what my wife's face will look like when I tell her I bought this product").

Two, they will move their eyes directly up and to the left when they are thinking about the past ("My husband showed his true colors when he found out how much I spent last year").

Three, when they are thinking in images, people also typically move their eyes in another way: They look straight ahead for a few seconds, and their eyes seem somewhat unfocused. The glazed expression does not mean a visual person isn't interested in what is going on, however. It merely means he or she is synthesizing thoughts—taking a few seconds to flip through that View-Master to let the thoughts sink in.

In my seminars, I tell my listeners to do the following exercise: Stand face-to-face with someone and ask some leading questions, using visual predicates. Inquire about the past ("Did your son beam when you gave him that car?" "What was the look on your wife's face when you told her you're buying that camcorder?"). Ask a question that requires thought of the future ("What do you see yourself doing in five years?"). Watch where the eyes go.

You'll notice that when you ask someone to think about the future in visual terms, their eyes go up right. When you ask them to visualize the past, their eyes go up left.

In a real sales situation, there is a lot happening, of course, and initially, you may be more worried about how you present yourself and your product than you are about your client's eye movements. But once you have practiced with a friend and gained some confidence, try it in an actual meeting. I have learned that most people begin reading eye movements in about one week.

To appreciate how powerful a tool this is for knowing what someone is really thinking, consider the following scenario: You are selling a car and are at the fun stage, when your customer is obviously interested in buying, but wants to get the best price possible. She says, "Well, I really love this car, but you know, I can get a better deal at Dealer X." "Oh," you ask, "what did he offer you?" "I can offer the same car for five hundred dollars less—with air conditioning thrown in for free."

Meanwhile, you watch her eyes. If she's looking up and to the right, she's lying. Why? She's thinking about the future, constructing images of things that have not yet happened. If she's really thinking about the past—her conversation with Dealer X— she'll be looking up and to the left. And you now have a good clue as to how you should proceed in the deal you offer her.

Once you get good at watching eye movements, you can use it to strengthen any negotiating position. CIA agents actually use this technique abroad when they don't have access to lie detectors. I even used it in watching the Anita Hill–Clarence Thomas hearings in the fall of 1991. Caught up in trying to figure out the truth, as everyone else in the country was, I used eye movement to form my opinion. My verdict? They were both lying.

In any courtroom, the accepted wisdom is that you catch lying by inconsistencies in what people say. I think it's much deeper and more subtle than that. You usually develop a sense of mistrust about a person. You form your opinions by paying attention both to what someone says and how that person behaves.

During the hearings, I noticed that when there were inconsistencies in Hill's or Thomas's testimony, they both looked up and to the right. Remember, looking up to the right is a sign that a person is creating images. For instance, Arlen Specter, the Senator from Pennsylvania, was very sharp in zeroing in on Anita Hill's testimony. At one point, he asked her why she waited seven years to come forward with her allegations. She said, "I want to protect other women," and looked up right. To me that indicated other motives. Perhaps she was really thinking, *I'm angry at the son of a bitch and want to get back at him!*

Clarence Thomas also had his share of half-truths. When Senator Howard Metzenbaum of Ohio asked Thomas whether he

VISUAL CUES

Predicates	Eye Movement	Visual Characteristics
see	up right (thinking about	maintains good eye contact
show	the future)	voice high-pitched, fast
bright	up left (thinking about	good with directions
picture	the past)	good visual memory
clear	unfocused/staring	
look	(synthesizing	
envision	thoughts—	
view	converting words to	
perceive	images)	
illustrate		
highlight		
focus		
reflect		
watch		
preview		
survey		
perspective		

had ever invited Ms. Hill on a date, Thomas said no, and looked up right. To me, that indicated that he certainly had, though perhaps not in the obscene language he was accused of having used.

Eye movements will not tell you the entire story, but they will confirm any hunch that something is up. Later on in the book, as I discuss various techniques of dealing with clients, I will show you how you can make your work more effective by checking and rechecking the truth of your customers' statements as you watch their eyes.

As far as Anita Hill and Clarence Thomas are concerned, I think Senator Joseph Biden, the chairman of the Judiciary Committee, said it best. When Dan Rather of CBS asked him what he had learned from the hearings, Biden answered, "I think one

VISUALS

A VISUAL WILL
MOVE HIS EYES ...

Up Right

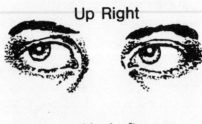

Up Left

Unfocused

of them was lying." It was a perfect comment for the entire episode.

The Auditories

In the late 1970s, I had the chance to play one of the best tennis champions on the face of the earth. His name was Jimmy Connors.

We played a first-round match at a tournament in the Midwest. Jimmy had one strategy with me: It was called "clean my clock," beating me 6–1, 6–2. I was embarrassed by such a lopsided loss, even if it was to such an outstanding champion. But afterward, I realized I should make my loss into a learning experience.

If you follow tennis, you probably realize that in his heyday, Jimmy Connors had the best return of serve in all of professional tennis. He was the only player on the tour who could return Roscoe Tanner's 138-mph serve for winners—meaning, Tanner never touched the ball.

I walked up to Jimmy and asked, "How do you return serves so effectively? Do you step in, bend your knees, roll to the balls of your feet? Do you block the shot back? Do you slice? Jimmy, give me a tip."

Jimmy Connors looked at me and said, "Kerry, I just made twenty-five thousand dollars off you in forty-five minutes. I guess you deserve an answer. I listen to the way the ball sounds as it comes off the server's racket. I can hear," he continued, "if the serve is a top spin, 'American Twist,' slice, flat serve. I can hear what the ball's gonna do. I move to the place in the court the ball will bounce. I then anticipate. It's point, game, set, match, Connors."

Jimmy Connors is an auditory. He *listens* to what is going on around him, and devises his strategy based on what he hears.

People whose mental map is primarily auditory make up about 25 percent of the population.

Auditories listen to the way you say things. Usually, they get more information from how you say something than they do from what you are actually saying. The way you deliver information—your voice pitch, pace, timbre, and intonation—means more to an auditory than anything else.

Think of auditories as having minds like jukeboxes, those wonderful music machines that we associate with the 1950s. You would put in a coin, push a letter-number combination, and a little arm inside the jukebox would reach up and over and grab a record. After the record was put on the turntable, a stylus came down and the selected song was played.

The auditory's mind works the same way. When he hears you speak, an auditory reaches for the appropriate "record," trying to get an idea of what you are talking about. When he finds the record and begins playing it, he has a reference point for your message. He suddenly comprehends your ideas.

What predicates does an auditory use? *Tone:* "Don't take that tone with me, young man," my mother used to say. *Static:* "All I ever get from you is a lot of static." *Rings:* "Hey, that rings a bell." *Sounds:* "Sounds good to me." *Say:* "Say, did you hear the one about . . . ?" *Tell:* "Can you tell me more about it? Can you tell me how it works?"

Auditories love the telephone. They sometimes get more business done on the phone than anywhere else, because they love to hear themselves and others talk. If someone tells you she prefers to do business by phone or doesn't really need to see you face-to-face, she is an auditory, a person who is most comfortable in the world of sound.

Auditories respond more directly to sounds than people who use other modes of thinking. I recently took a plane flight across the country and sat next to a woman who looked like a first-time flier. As the plane took off, I noticed that she was so frightened, her knuckles were turning white from grasping the armrest. But after a half hour in the air, she became more relaxed and started looking around as if she wanted to call the flight attendant for something.

As she looked up, I saw her notice the call button on the ceiling. She reached up, pushed it, and it went *ding*. The woman immediately said, "Can I have a cup of coffee?" There wasn't a flight attendant in sight. She had obviously responded to the sound of the button rather than to anything else, and began speaking as if on cue.

Often, auditories say things they don't mean to say. They actually need to hear their words in order to understand what they're saying. By then, it's too late to stop.

Do you know someone who mumbles or likes to talk to himself? That's another very auditory characteristic. "Hi, Kerry. How are you? Well, I'm fine. I think I'm going to do OK." We used to think this was a sign of some sort of emotional disturbance. Now, we label this kind of behavior self-talk, a perfectly legitimate way to solve problems by talking them through, aloud. Tennis-great Billie Jean King was famous for doing that during tough match situations.

Auditories have breathing and speech patterns that are different from visuals. Visually based people, not concerned with how they use sound because they are too busy creating pictures and focusing on images, speak very quickly. Breathing fast and high in the chest, they also tend to have voices that are more high-pitched. Auditories, on the other hand, try very hard to sound good most of the time. So they will speak rhythmically and deliberately, conscious of every word. Their breathing is similar—slower and deeper than that of visuals.

Some psychology researchers even believe that you can determine whether a person is thinking auditorially, because such people will touch their faces as they listen to you. Next time you see someone talking to you with a hand up to his or her face, try to notice whether the eyes are positioned side right, side left, or down left. If the answer is yes to any of these positions, you are speaking to an auditory.

AUDITORY CUES

Predicates	Eye Movements	Auditory Characteristics
say	side right (thinking about	lower-pitched voice,
tell	the future)	rhythmic and smooth
tone	side left (thinking about	they try to sound good
static	the past)	like concerts and music
ring	down left (synthesizing	talk to themselves
sound	thoughts—converting	
speak	words to sounds)	
express		
mention		
accent		
resonate		
remark		
ask		
inquire		
hear		
talk		

Eye Movements in the Auditory Mode

When people think in an auditory mode, they move their eyes in certain directions, just as when they are thinking visually. But instead of looking up in either direction or staring straight ahead, they look to the side, either right or left. When they are looking to the right, chances are they are thinking about future information ("I wonder what my wife will say when she hears that I bought this"; "I wonder if my accountant will laugh when he finds out how much I made last year").

When moving their eyes side left, people in an auditory mode are thinking about the past. If you asked a prospective client a question such as, "Tell me, how much money did you pay last

36

AUDITORIES

AN AUDITORY WILL
MOVE HIS EYES . . .

Side Right

Side Left

Down Left

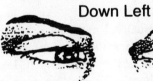

year in taxes?'' your client will tend to look side left as he tries to remember a conversation he had with his accountant.

People in an auditory mode move their eyes in another way that is very typical: looking directly down and to the left. They are trying to make sense of what you are saying. They are, in effect, talking to themselves, processing all the sounds, trying to compare what you are saying to what they have heard before. When your client looks down left, stop talking. Allow some time for his internal conversation to play itself out. If you continue talking, he won't hear you.

The Kinesthetics

I was introduced to hockey great Wayne Gretzky a number of years ago. After complimenting him on his ice performance that day, I told him that I was doing research into sports behavior, and asked him about his technique. ''I saw you hit shots into the goal on one skate,'' I said. ''I saw you hit shots between your legs with one hand. How do you do that? What goes through your mind? I'd like to know what you are thinking about right before you make that outstanding shot.''

Gretzky responded: ''Usually, I'm double or triple teamed by our opponents. They key on me as the guy to beat. But no matter how many players are on me, if I'm near the goal, I suddenly get this feeling in my stomach, this visceral gut feeling that says, 'Wayne, shoot the puck.' If I get that feeling, the puck goes in.''

Wayne Gretzky is a kinesthetic, someone who acts on what he *feels*. This is very different from the pictures Dan Fouts would make or the sounds that Jimmy Connors hears. Gretzky gets a feeling and then he makes a shot, usually a game-winning one.

Kinesthetics—I call them *kinos* for short—make up about 40 percent of the population. These people get information primarily from touch, emotions, gut instincts, and hunches. They often get goose bumps. They buy on the basis of how they feel, and make quick judgments about whether they like or dislike someone. Before they can give you their trust, they need to get some kind of feeling that tells them its OK to do so.

When I speak around the country, I find there are a lot of audience members who want to hear about my family. I suspect the people who care most about this are kinos. When I tell an anecdote about my wife or children, I can just see certain audience members perk up. The anecdote has allowed them to develop a quick feeling of trust toward me.

The words that kinesthetics use face-to-face or on the telephone are very much oriented toward emotions and the body. *Feel:* "Here's how I feel about what you just said." *Grab:* "How does that grab you?" *Touch base:* "Let's touch base next week." *Handle:* "Let me see if I can get a handle on that." *Rub:* "It rubs me the wrong way." A visual will say, "Here's my view." The auditory will say, "Here's how it sounds to me." On the other hand, the kinesthetic will say, "Here's my feeling on that. I've got a good grasp on it. Here's my impression."

Bill Clinton is a kinesthetic. Just think of all those long, rather unwieldy speeches where he talks about caring and feelings. And what was his first public ceremony right after the inauguration? He stood for hours waiting to hug and shake hands with the hundreds of well-wishers who trooped through the White House. All presidents have to at least make a show of mingling with the public. Bill Clinton really loves pressing the flesh.

It takes kinesthetics a few moments longer to access a feeling than it does for a visual to create a picture or for an auditory to create a sound. For this reason, they appear to think more slowly. This misperception can create problems. A colleague once told me that he didn't like selling to kinesthetics, because they "didn't think in the right way." He thought they weren't as bright as those in the other two groups.

Have you ever seen news clips of Albert Einstein being interviewed? When asked about his theories, where did his eyes go? Down and to the right. Einstein was a kinesthetic, and would rarely make eye contact with a camera. He came up with the Theory of Relativity, imagining what it might feel like to ride a beam of light through the universe. One could say he discovered the Theory of Relativity by feeling it.

Kinesthetics have a number of other characteristics that will let you know very quickly that these people are thinking with their feelings. Research shows that kinesthetics make frequent pauses in their conversations. If I ask a customer, "What do you think about this computer so far?" the typical kinesthetic will respond: "Well, I think that . . . mmm . . . what you're saying to me right now has a lot of . . . uh . . . merit. And . . . uh . . . frankly . . . uh . . . I feel that I have a good grasp on how it works . . . ." People who talk with frequent pauses are trying to get a feeling. They are thinking, *How do I feel about what he just asked me*? When they get their feeling, they are able to continue talking.

Kinesthetics also love to touch people and things. Such individuals often touch you to make a point—on the arm, on the shoulder, even on the back. When you are talking with them across a desk, they are often playing with small objects they seem to pick up without thinking: pens, paper clips, erasers, pieces of paper. Touching gives them a feeling of connectedness.

Kinesthetics are also likely to feel temperature changes more quickly than auditories or visuals. Almost every meeting planner and program chairman in America knows that if a room is too hot or too cold, the audience will have trouble listening to the speaker. All of us need to be comfortable physically in order to concentrate. If someone is particularly picky about temperature or sensitive to its changes and lets you know about it, it is an indication that the person is kinesthetic.

I have often accompanied salespersons on their business calls to study their interactions with prospective clients. Very often, I have watched clients offer them coffee, Coke, cookies, or something else to eat or drink. In almost every case, the inexperienced salespersons refuse the offer, probably thinking it somehow unprofessional. This is a huge mistake. By accepting the client's hospitality, the salesperson is saying, "I respect you. I enjoy being here. I would like to partake of your graciousness." If the client's hospitality is not accepted, he or she automatically feels discomfort at having been refused.

While kinesthetics may interpret such action most negatively, feeling comfortable and accepted is important for all of us. Never refuse a client's hospitality, whether in someone's home or office. It is one of those small gestures that doesn't take any effort on your part, and yet does a lot in creating an atmosphere of trust.

Kinesthetic Eye Movement

Have you ever heard the expression, "Boy, he was downright mean"? This phrase came about largely because people were looking down, to the right, and experiencing some sort of intense emotion. This is the one predominant eye movement when someone is accessing feelings: down and to the right.

Whenever I speak in front of groups, I bring a person up to the front of the room. I turn the person toward the audience, and massage his or her shoulders. This person is usually very self-conscious at the beginning. But the more I massage, the more relaxed the person becomes. Then I ask the participant to concentrate only on the shoulders—that is, what is being felt—to induce a feeling mode. Inevitably, having forgotten about the rest of the audience and thinking only about the massage, participants look down and to the right.

I still remember a very interesting incident that occurred during the vice presidential debates in 1984, showing how easily kinesthetic eye movement can be misinterpreted. The consensus among newscasters was that George Bush was more charismatic and articulate in front of the television cameras than his opponent,

Geraldine Ferraro. I still wonder, however, how much that interpretation had to do with the fact that Ms. Ferraro made some big mistakes in front of the camera.

During the course of the debate, reporters directed questions to each candidate. When the questions were directed at George Bush, he would look directly into the camera and then become unfocused, staring blankly for a few seconds as a visual-mode person would while he thought of an answer. Then he looked directly into the camera again. The TV viewing audience never realized that George Bush broke eye contact to think.

And what did Geraldine Ferraro do? She looked down to the right like a kinesthetic, and completely lost eye contact with the cameras. She did this continually, looking down at the podium after each question was asked.

Watching the debates in my living room, I overheard Dan Rather of CBS ask his colleague Morley Safer, "How come she's looking down so much?" "I don't know, Dan," Safer answered. "There aren't any notes in front of her. Nothing to look at."

The point is, Ms. Ferraro wasn't reading anything. She's a kinesthetic. That's the only way she could think, looking down and to the right. The problem was, the country didn't understand her thought process. Many people thought she was trying to hide something. This perception seemed to dog her in her unsuccessful race for a New York Senate seat in 1992. How much of her loss was due to the fact that people couldn't trust her because of the allegations about her husband's ties to organized crime, and how much of it was due to her on-camera manner?

When someone is looking down to the right, feelings are being accessed. Give such persons some time to respond. You haven't lost them—they are just trying to understand what they feel about a particular situation.

KINESTHETIC CUES

Predicates	Eye Movement	Kinesthetic Characteristics
feel	down right (synthesizing	feel hot or cold about you
grab	thoughts—	frequent pauses in
touch	converting words to	conversation
handle	feelings)	like to touch people
rub		
grasp		
affect		
impress		
hit		
suffer		
tackle		
pressure		
know		
intuit		

KINESTHETICS

A KINESTHETIC WILL
MOVE HIS EYES . . .

Down Right

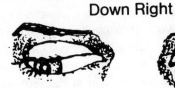

What Is Your Mental Map?

If you aren't communicating to your clients in their preferred mode, you are in danger of talking at cross purposes. To show how important this is, I always point to a great scene in the hit movie *Ghostbusters*.

In this film, Dan Aykroyd and Bill Murray play two professors trying to rid the world of ghosts. In one of the first scenes of the movie, they are walking through a ghost-ridden library where books have been stacked strangely and cards have begun flying out of slime-clogged files. Suddenly, stopping his fellow ghost-busters, Dan Aykroyd says, "Listen, did you *smell* that?" Does this make sense? It's like saying to your client, "How's that sound to you?" and your client looks up at the ceiling thinking, "I don't see a thing."

Be aware of your preferred mode of communicating to avoid the same kind of confusion. Here are a few exercises to determine your own mental map:

Find a partner, someone you know fairly well, and tell that person about your first hour of wakefulness this morning. Describe what happened. As you are talking about what you remember, try to do it in stages, first describing what you saw, then what you heard, and finally, what you felt.

You will quickly realize that your favorite system is the one that comes most easily to you and the one about which you have the most memories. If you are strongly oriented to one mode, you may even find it very difficult to remember anything in the other modes. Test yourself in the same way by describing your last vacation. I often use this method at the seminars I teach, and it is truly amazing to see people gravitate to a preferred mode. The words come out, one after the other, very specific, very descriptive. Sometimes, I intentionally ask a question that requires thought in one of the other modes, and the person becomes very self-conscious, unable to remember anything. It's almost as if the person's brains have shut down, needing time to readjust.

Are you better with faces than you are with names? This is a very visual characteristic. I was on an airplane recently and sat next to someone who swore he recognized me. He said, "I know you. Your name is, uh . . . your name is uh . . ." I said, "Kerry Johnson." He replied, "No, that's not it."

Are you a good speller? If you are, you are probably a visual. Visuals are good spellers because they actually picture the entire word as they spell it out. A person who is auditory, for example, focuses on its sound and spells it phonetically instead, which usually is incorrect.

Here is a quick test to determine whether you have auditory characteristics. Please complete the following sentence: "7UP is the Un____" You probably thought *cola*. The question is, did you see a picture of the word *cola*, or did you hear the sound? If you heard the sound, you are probably an auditory, or at least were thinking in that mode when completing the question.

Are you the kind of person who goes around the office giving back rubs and shoulder massages to everyone? That's a very kinesthetic quality. If you're big on hugging or touching people or slapping them on the back to say hello, that's another sign that your primary mode is kinesthetic.

Knowing which way you communicate most naturally will make you that much more effective when you go to call on clients. You can start to develop some strategies to make sure that you and your clients aren't speaking at cross purposes. You may also be able to figure out why certain calls in the past have gone badly, and try to approach those same clients again.

Below is the Preference Survey we have developed at International Productivity Systems. Take the test to find out what your preferred mode of thinking is. There are no right or wrong answers to this test. Very simply, the mode you score highest in is your favorite. The mode you score lowest in is your least favorite, although you can communicate in all three modes.

VISUAL/AUDITORY/KINESTHETIC
PREFERENCE SURVEY

Each individual has one primary mode in which he or she prefers to communicate—either visual, auditory, or kinesthetic. However, we also have the ability to move from one mode to another, depending on the situation. For example, if you are right-handed, you probably would rather write with the right hand than the left. You may have ability to write with the left, but comfort lies with the right.

In the list below, check A, B, or C next to the response that most appeals to you. This will help you determine whether your predominant mode is visual, auditory, or kinesthetic. There are no correct or incorrect answers; you are simply indicating your preferences. The mode that you score highest in indicates your perceptual preference. A signifies the auditory mode, B the visual mode and C the kinesthetic mode.

1.   A _____   I love to listen to music.
     B _____   I enjoy art galleries and window shopping.
     C _____   I feel compelled to dance to good music.

2.   A _____   I would rather take an oral test than a written
                   test.
     B _____   I was good at spelling in school.
     C _____   I tend to answer test questions using my "gut"
                   feelings.

3.   A _____   I've been told I have a great speaking voice.
     B _____   My confidence increases when I look good.
     C _____   I enjoy being touched.

4.   A _____   I can resolve problems more quickly when I
                   talk out loud.

B _____ I would rather be shown an illustration than have something explained to me.

C _____ I find myself holding or touching things as they are being explained.

5. A _____ I can usually determine sincerity by the sound of a person's voice.

B _____ I find myself evaluating others based on their appearance.

C _____ The way others shake hands with me means a lot to me.

6. A _____ I would rather listen to cassettes than read books.

B _____ I like to watch television and go to the movies.

C _____ I like hiking and other outdoor activities.

7. A _____ I can hear even the slightest noise that my car makes.

B _____ It's important that my car is kept clean, inside and out.

C _____ I like a car that feels good when I drive it.

8. A _____ Others tell me that I'm easy to talk to.

B _____ I enjoy "people watching."

C _____ I tend to touch people when talking.

9. A _____ I am aware of what voices sound like on the phone, as well as face-to-face.

B _____ I often remember what someone looked like, but not the person's name.

C _____ I can't remember what people look like.

10. A _____ I often find myself humming or singing to the radio.

B _____ I enjoy photography.

C _____ I like to make things with my hands.

11. A _____ I would rather have an idea explained to me than read it.

B _____ I enjoy speakers more if they use visual aids.

C _____ I like to participate in activities rather than watch.

12. A _____ I am a good listener.

B _____ I find myself evaluating others based on their appearance.

C _____ I feel positive or negative toward others, sometimes without knowing why.

13. A _____ I can resolve problems more quickly when I talk out loud.

B _____ I am good at finding my way using a map.

C _____ I exercise because of the way I feel afterward.

14. A _____ I like a house with rooms that allow for quiet areas.

B _____ It's important that my house is clean and tidy.

C _____ I like a house that feels comfortable.

15. A _____ I like to try to imitate the way people talk.

B _____ I make a list of things I need to do each day.

C _____ I've been told that I'm well-coordinated.

Count the total number of *A* responses, *B* responses, and *C* responses and note below.

Your score: _____ Number of *A* responses

_____ Number of *B* responses

_____ Number of *C* responses

If you scored most *A* responses, it indicates an *auditory* preference. If you scored most *B* responses, it indicates a *visual* preference. If you scored most *C* responses, it indicates a *kinesthetic* preference.

My perceptual preference, based on this questionnaire, is

_____ .

Rapport is the bridge that helps the person you are communicating with find meaning and intent in the things you say.

CHAPTER TWO

Establishing Rapport: The Key to Big Money

Ron Rice mixed his first batch of Hawaiian Tropic suntan lotion in his garage in 1966. Now, Hawaiian Tropic is a multimillion-dollar company, and the former lifeguard is a business tycoon. Once dubbed the Hugh Hefner of Daytona Beach, the high-living Mr. Rice was asked in an interview to what he attributed his success. He responded that in addition to hard work, it was "reading people and understanding human nature."

What is reading people and understanding human nature? It is knowing how to establish rapport. If you develop rapport with others, opportunities will come your way and favorable situations will present themselves to you without your having to go after them. Rapport creates a feeling of trust, and people gravitate toward those whom they trust. If you have poor rapport skills, people will avoid you.

This is true in almost all of our relationships—from business, to marriage, to personal one-on-one communication. Rapport is the bridge that helps the person you are communicating with find meaning and intent in the things you say. It helps someone feel comfortable with you and it creates a feeling of warmth and understanding. Most important, when it comes to selling, rapport will help your prospective customers feel that what you're saying is directed right at them, aimed at their particular needs and desires. It is what convinces them to buy from you.

We define rapport simply as a relation marked by harmony, conformity, accord, or affinity. Without rapport, you're just communicating information. You might as well just read your sales presentation to a customer. If you can't establish that bridge of trust, chances are you won't make a sale.

One of the million-dollar salespeople I've studied once told me that when a client resists her, she knows that rapport is too low. It also shows her that she is doing something wrong. To this million-dollar seller, lack of rapport means that she hasn't yet found the appropriate method with which to communicate to her client. She hasn't found a way to help her client identify and work with her.

This woman's emphasis on what she might be doing wrong and not on how badly or ineptly her clients behave underscores two qualities that are part of every salesperson's ability to build rapport successfully. They are caring and being flexible.

Caring is the binding force in a buyer-seller relationship. It is the attitude that you bring to the relationship; it's what changes it from an adversarial one into one of communication. It is a genuine desire to learn about your client's needs and how best to fulfill them. No technique I can show you will work unless your clients know, as motivational speaker Zig Ziglar puts it, how much you care.

What does it mean to care? In the first place, it means you are sincere in your motives. You don't lie, pretending that your motives in selling are something other than what they are. You are selling because this is your livelihood. You enjoy doing it and doing it well, and you want to do the best you can. Don't pretend otherwise.

There is a concept in negotiation that works very well, which is called Win/Win. Instead of looking at negotiating as a competition, where one person is destined to win and the other to lose, the concept of Win/Win says that *both* parties can benefit. If this open attitude is present, the negotiation process goes much more smoothly, and both parties end up being pleased.

The same is true in sales. If you let your customers know what you want and what will make you win, they will help you win—as long as they know you're doing the same for them. There is nothing wrong with telling your customers that you want a commission for a job well done, for example, if at the same time you assure them that you are doing your level best to help them get what they want.

There is a difference between being sincere and being Pollyanna. By caring about a client, I don't mean you have to overlook someone's faults. Accept them—and focus on something else that you feel positive about.

Accompanying an insurance salesman on his rounds one day, I began talking to him about his next client, a high-powered banker who could be very abusive and noncommittal. "Oh, he's such a jerk," the salesman told me as we approached his house. "It's all I can do to smile and shake hands with him."

The salesman did smile—he tried smiling throughout the entire meeting, but the more he smiled, the less rapport there was between him and the banker. I could see that although he was negative and at times curt, the banker was also very sharp and enjoyed the give-and-take of the discussion about financial matters. If the salesman had been able to accept his dislike of the banker's personality and instead focus on the banker's knowledge, he might have begun to develop some positive communication. He might have even found an occasion or two to smile sincerely. Instead, his lack of rapport cost him the sale.

How much you care also comes across in your dependability, showing your clients that you can deliver what you promise. Don't expect to go far in sales with the attitude that you can cut corners or sell on false or inflated pretenses. It may get you a sale in the short run, but will lose clients in the long run. As a matter of fact, I have found that referrals make up approximately 90 percent of my income.

I think of a salesperson as a problem solver. Too few salespeople try to solve their clients' problems. Those who do become supersellers. Your clients are not concerned with how good or inexpensive or new-fangled your product is if it doesn't fulfill their specific requirements. If you approach your sales presentations with the attitude that you are there to find out how best you can do this—that you are there to understand rather than to manipulate—your clients will sense this attitude and will be more open to the service or product you are selling.

The other quality that is so important in building rapport is *flexibility*. Think of flexibility as having ready access to many behavioral tools, tools that help you see your client's point of view. Having flexibility helps you work *with* your clients, rather than selling *at* them or *to* them.

With high flexibility, you are able to deal with people as they wish to be dealt with. You are able to break the golden rule: *Instead of treating people the way you want to be treated, treat people the way they want to be treated.* By communicating with them in their unique style, you will be able to reach a higher level of rapport more quickly.

An inability to be flexible can cost you sales and create missed opportunities. I attended a cocktail party a couple of years ago and began talking to a gentleman about his business. I am always looking for opportunities to talk with business owners and managers about what their problems are and if I can be of help to them. This man, for example, produced pipeline hardware for oil companies. He may have benefited from inviting me to give a sales seminar at his company or speak at a conference at which his sales staff would be present.

Unfortunately, the man didn't seem very interested in our conversation. Although he kept talking with me, he refused to make eye contact. He turned his head from side to side while looking around the room. He seemed to be looking aggressively for other opportunities to market himself.

I found myself getting more and more annoyed, not liking this man's manner at all. Even though it occurred to me that maybe I was doing something wrong by not grabbing this person's attention sufficiently, I didn't do anything to change the situation. I was so upset by his behavior, I spent all my energy thinking about how much this man was offending me.

If I had been more flexible, watching out for his cues, listening to what he was really saying, I may have been able to make a sale. And if not a sale, perhaps a referral or a new opportunity to speak with one of his colleagues. The point is, I didn't get beyond first base to find out. I didn't even begin building rapport.

In the first chapter, we discussed how your clients may have a different understanding of the world from yours, and how they want you to communicate with them in their own unique style. Be open to this reality. Instead of letting it be an impediment, be flexible enough to use it as an opportunity.

Selling to Visuals

You learned which of your clients were visuals by the visual words, or predicates, they used in talking about themselves. Use these same words yourself. When visuals hear words such as *show*, *clear*, *see*, *bright*, *picture*, *perspective*, and *view*, they understand you more quickly, because they don't have to take those extra moments to translate what you are saying into images. You've done the translating for them. And just by talking in someone's preferred mode, you are building rapport because you are communicating that you understand that person. The fact that all this is happening at an unconscious level makes it all the more effective.

For example, if you are in a situation selling real estate, here's how you would talk to a visual: "Jim, can't you just picture your family all sitting together in this lovely dining room? I'll bet you can see how all the furniture will look when we fill this room up.

Notice how bright it is with all these windows." Because you use visually based words and point out visually appealing aspects of your product, your client trusts you as somebody who knows what he or she is experiencing. If you were seeing an accountant, you would likely present numbers to him. If this person is a visual, he wants pictures more than numbers.

I know a saleswoman who makes more than a million dollars a year in commission selling financial products. This is how she sells to her visual prospects: "What do you see yourself accomplishing as a result of being with me today?"—note *see yourself accomplishing*. The clients' eyes go right up to the ceiling as they picture just what it is they have in mind.

This is so important, I can't press the point too often. If you can communicate with your clients in their own mode, they will buy much more quickly from you. You are going to gain their trust more quickly, communicate more meaningfully, and get more business accomplished.

Recently, a colleague whom I'll call Larry told me how he got one of the biggest accounts of the year for his company. As a partner in a "big-six" accounting firm, he received a telephone call from a credit union executive who asked that he speak on new tax proposals at a convention of the credit union's members. Larry knew that if he got to speak at this convention, his accounting firm would receive a great amount of business later because of the huge number of attendees expected.

In discussing his proposal with Larry, the credit union executive said such things as, "I'd like to see what you can offer"; "I'd like you to give me a picture of how you would do the presentation"; "I have interviewed numerous firms for this job, but I'd like to get your perspective on how you would handle this assignment." The executive was obviously a visual.

Larry understood that he needed to use just the right words, at the right time, to attract the credit union executive's interest. He knew the executive would be worried about the more complex tax issues, which needed adequate explanation. He turned the problem into the solution, emphasizing its visual aspects. In his response to the executive, he used the following examples: "We use gorgeous blue handouts with gold borders so the attendees can take something home from the presentation. We also use a projection system that transfers vivid numbers and graphs from a computer onto a screen. This will really look dazzling, but will make things simple and clear at the same time. Everyone will easily see how much they can benefit from these tax proposals, and get a perspective on how their businesses will profit as well."

The credit union executive liked Larry's solution, telling him, "I can see what you're saying." He could *see* what he had heard.

When Larry asked him when he would like to follow up on the matter, the executive told him he didn't need to do more interviewing. "I have such a good picture of what you'll do that I think you're the one." The phone call took Larry about ten minutes, in what probably would have taken about fifteen or twenty. And he saved himself numerous follow-up calls as well.

Had Larry not realized that this executive was a visual, rapport would not have been generated as quickly, and he would have had to work much harder to get the speaking engagement.

What we are talking about here is having an edge—by communicating to your clients in their preferred mode, you gain time and have an advantage that you otherwise would not have. When you get used to using such techniques automatically, you will literally cut your selling time by half and increase your sales enormously.

In addition to using visual predicates, always keep brochures, graphs, and pictures handy when selling to visuals. Any concept will be much more quickly understood if you can show a bar chart or a graph while you speak. If your product line happens to be a tangible object, produce an example, if possible. The maxim, "Show, don't tell," is particularly apt in the case of visually based people.

And draw pictures. One of the biggest sales hitters I know sells life insurance by discussing forced savings plans, plans that lock people into saving money. You wouldn't think such a topic easily lends itself to visual images. But every time this salesperson talks, he illustrates his points by drawing little pie charts and bar graphs. It's a simple technique that works just for that reason. The salesperson draws a slice of the pie to show his client how much he or she might be paying in taxes. Then he might make another slice to show disposable income. The client understands much more quickly, because he doesn't have to do any translating from numbers to pictures.

Don't forget to use your hands when you are talking to visuals. Get them to see things by painting pictures in the air, not just on paper. This is especially useful when you are selling a concept rather than something tangible. You can use your hands to punctuate your descriptions of the product and its benefits, giving your clients a better idea of what you are talking about.

Selling to Auditories

"How does this sound so far?" "Does this ring a bell with you?" "Can you tell why this is more efficient?" Auditory predicates let auditories know that you are speaking in their language; hearing them, they will relax and open up to you.

When you are selling to auditories, remember to stress the auditory qualities your product may have. If you are in real estate, for example, and are selling a house that has a creek in the backyard, stress how nice the creek sounds or simply how quiet the neighborhood is. If you are selling a car, point out how smoothly the engine hums. If you put your mind to it, you can find pleasing auditory qualities in many products. Pointing out that little something might be just enough to grab someone's fancy and stimulate real interest in your product.

Because auditories are so deeply affected by what they hear, why not tickle their ears? Television minister Robert Schuller of the Crystal Cathedral commands the ears of millions every Sunday morning. He doesn't use slides or illustrations. His great tool is his voice. He says, "What the mind can conceive and believe, it will achieve." Whether you agree or disagree with his philosophy, that kind of sentence certainly grabs your attention because it sounds so good. My life insurance agent once said to me, "Kerry, if you die without enough insurance, you are going to leave your wife financially dejected, abjected, and rejected." The way he said it sounded so terrible, I bought the insurance.

What gave Ross Perot such a big boost when he reentered the presidential race in October 1992? It was his use of words. Although Mr. Perot has a reputation for being plain speaking, he actually loves word play. Here are some of the comments he made during the first presidential debate, which got him off and running again: On an opponent's view of converting defense-oriented industries to civilian ones: "He didn't care whether we made potato chips or computer chips." On the harshness of his proposals to cut the deficit: "I'm not playing Lawrence Welk music tonight." On the economy: "We're sitting on a ticking time bomb, folks." On Washington: "This is a town where the White House says, 'Congress did it.' Congress says, 'The White House did it.' Then, when they get off by themselves, they said, 'Nobody did it.' "

Notice that all of the above examples are auditory ones. They were effective because they were so clear and simple, which was exactly the image that Perot wanted to present. At one point, when a journalist asked him how he would get Congress to pass all of his proposals, he answered, "We're gonna *make* them do it." When you think about it, that's a pretty inane comment—no one can *make* Congress do anything. Yet everyone loved it, not because they believed it was true, but because Perot was hitting a deep nerve. They wanted simplicity, not George Bush's Ivy League demeanor or Bill Clinton's slick tone. It wasn't the content of his message that got Perot 19 percent of the vote in

November—it was more the meaning behind the message and his intent in delivering it.

Besides words, there are other auditory aids you can use. Music for one. If you are meeting a client in your office, don't forget how useful music can be. Music has an effect both on emotions and behavior. It can disturb as well as soothe. Auditories, of course, are particularly sensitive to it.

Corporate America has used music to influence people for years. The Muzak Corporation says that its music can increase factory productivity by 17 percent. The company claims it can increase clerical performance in the office by 13.5 percent, and that Muzak will reduce turnover in staff by 53 percent. In a study done at Loyola University, it was found that the speed of music played in supermarkets influenced buying. When the music was slow, sales were 38.2 percent higher than when fast music was played. Interestingly enough, when shoppers were asked what they thought about the music, 33 percent didn't know what kind of music had been played, and 39 percent denied there was any music at all. The music had done its work on an unconscious level.

Studies also show that slow music causes us to relax and buy on impulse. This is particularly true in department stores, where we typically go to buy a specific product. When the music is fast, people tend to move more quickly, focus on what they want to buy, and then leave. When the music is slower, however, its soothing effect makes it easier for the consumer's attention to drift, as he or she notices other products instead of running out the door. If they see something they like, they are more prone to buy it.

Another auditory technique that can tap hidden markets is the use of audiotapes. I know a salesperson in southern California who uses audiotapes to introduce himself to prospective clients. He discusses the background of his company, includes testimonials from his previous clients on the tape, and then mails it out. With this tape he is able to get the attention of those people who would not be inclined to read a prospectus or go over a résumé.

We discussed how important it is to use illustrations and have brochures handy for visuals. Auditories like illustrative material, too, but this is how they prefer you handle it: Give them a piece of paper or an illustration, wait twelve seconds, and then explain it out loud. The twelve seconds gives auditories time to orient themselves and get a reference point for what they are looking at. Then they want to hear it from you.

We have noticed that when we give auditories a page of text, they will look at the words across the top. They will also look down the left side of the sheet and at a few things in the middle, but they will not try to read the entire thing or get more information from it. After about twelve seconds they need you to explain what they just got through seeing.

Since visuals get more information from what they see than from what they hear, give them the sheet of paper, and keep quiet. Don't say a word until they make eye contact again.

Selling to Kinesthetics

You want to talk to kinesthetics in ways that directly address what they are feeling. Throughout your presentation, use statements such as the following: "Stan, what's your sense of this?" "Susan, our customer-service staff is available whenever you want to touch base." "Debbie, how does this grab you so far?" "Clark, what's your impression of these unique features?" All these statements "go for the gut." Kinesthetics will know what you are asking them because they know exactly what they feel. And they are able to give you feedback much more quickly.

To start building rapport at the very beginning, you can say the following: "What do you feel you would like to accomplish as a result of our meeting today?" or "Do you have a concrete idea of what you are looking for?" Notice how effective such questions are. They not only build rapport because of the kinesthetic predicates you use, they also provide you with a wealth of information from the feedback you get.

Give kinesthetics things to touch. If you do so, you'll be able to sell them five times faster. If you're selling a computer with a mouse, let them hold the mouse and feel it glide along the table-top. If you're selling a piece of furniture, let them feel its texture. And don't be afraid to use your imagination. If you're selling cars, for example, think of all the different surfaces you can let them touch: the seats, the stick shift, the various dashboard controls, the body. And don't forget the tires. Why do you think it is we kick the tires when we're buying a car? It satisfies the kinesthetic in all of us.

Don't forget how important touch is when you are using brochures or other illustrative materials. Instead of just showing a brochure to your clients, make sure they can hold it. Although they may look at the pictures or listen to your explanations about what the brochures contain, what is really important to them is that they have these materials in hand. Then they'll believe you.

Forgetting to do this can result in lost time or even a lost sale. A friend who is a dentist and knows my work once told me what happened to her at a convention. She was walking around the convention floor, where salespeople were showing off the latest technology for various dental procedures. At one booth, a salesman was discussing new plugs that were being used in making false teeth. He held one plug in his hand, demonstrating how the procedure would work. She thought it was a great idea and reached for the plug so that she could inspect it further. But the salesman was so caught up in his product, every time he was about to hand it to her, he snatched it back, remembering yet another advantage to it. She told me this happened about three or four times, until tired and frustrated, she left. "All I wanted to do was hold the thing for a few seconds," she told me later, laughing. "It took me another half a year before I got around to it again." By not being aware of how important it was for her to hold that little plug, the salesman lost a sale.

If you can make your point with a physical action of some kind, such as a touch or a gesture, you will really "grab" a kinesthetic's attention. Although I'm primarily an auditory, I also have a very strong kinesthetic side. I was a speaker at a major sales meeting a couple of years ago. A representative for a financial planning firm approached me as I was having dinner the night before. He said, "Kerry, you're a pretty big hitter, and a dollar means a lot to you, doesn't it?" More interested in the speech I was to give than in what he had to say, I replied, "Yeah, well—I work as hard as anybody." He continued, "You probably pay too much in taxes, don't you?" I agreed with that. Then he asked me to give him a dollar, which I did. "Kerry," he went on, "every time you make a dollar, the government takes your hard-earned buck. . . ." I didn't see what he was getting at and wanted to go back to my dinner, but he kept on talking. "Kerry, the government glares at you with that mischievous, greedy grin the IRS has, and then they take your hard-earned dollar and slowly rip that dollar bill right in front of your face." As he talked, he ripped my dollar bill in half. Right in front of me.

I was angry, even though he later gave me a dollar back. But guess what he got me to do? He got me to feel what he was talking about. That rip really made me realize what he wanted me to understand about government and taxes. Now, I don't want you to go around ripping dollar bills. But to me, it was a perfect example of what a powerful tool you have when you can link feelings with a particular action.

If you are selling to more than one person, you may well have to use more than one mode at a time. This is where your flexibility will really be put to the test. In our studies, we have found that a common mistake salespeople make in such situations is to unconsciously favor one person or the other—usually the person who shares one's own mental map. If the one being ignored has a say in whether or not to buy, that person very often sabotages the sale, simply for having been inadequately communicated with by the salesperson. Because rapport is not felt with the salesperson, reasons are found for not buying the product.

I was recently involved in a meeting in which a brokerage-house representative was discussing a retirement plan with a couple. Both the broker and the husband were visuals, while the wife was a kinesthetic. The broker developed very high rapport with the husband, constantly using visual predicates. But at the same time, he totally alienated the wife, who seemed more and more lost and upset as the meeting progressed.

Needless to say, the broker did not get very far in convincing the couple that his company would do a good job in investing their money. The wife continued to focus on potential problems, quibbling with the safety of the assets, the amount of money they would have to live on every month, with everything that could go wrong. She even said at one point, "I don't know, it just doesn't feel right to me." After sitting in the office with the couple for over an hour, the best the salesman could do was get them to promise to "think about it"—words we salespeople don't like to hear.

If the broker knew what you know now, here's how some of the conversation would have gone:

Salesperson:	John, how does this investment portfolio look to you so far?
John:	It looks OK to me.
Salesperson:	And you, Katherine? How do you feel about it?
Katherine:	I don't know . . . I guess I'm just not comfortable with the risk we'd be taking with some of these mutual funds. I know there's always some risk . . . .
Salesperson:	Here (handing her a brochure), take this—it will give you a better handle on what I'm talking about.
John:	My wife does bring up a good point,

	though. I worry about risk, too. How speculative is it?
Salesperson:	Why don't you take a look at this brochure, too, John (giving him a brochure as well). This will give you a better picture of our investment strategy and a clearer idea of our goals. Katherine, let me point out a few things in the chart on page two. It will give you a better feeling for how our funds have done over the long term. Because of your concern for safety and, John, your view of lowering the risk/return, I recommend this fund.

Notice how the broker kept going back and forth from one person to the other, while speaking in the appropriate mode. By making Katherine feel included every step of the way, he is lessening the chances for her sabotaging the sale. Notice also how easy it was for John to pick up on Katherine's negativity, and how important it was for the broker to immediately switch back to visual terms. This flexibility is what keeps the rapport building throughout the entire exchange.

People often ask me whether repeating the predicates a client uses ever becomes obvious. My answer is no. People are so consumed with themselves, with how they want to appear or what they want to tell you, they aren't really aware of what you're doing.

To illustrate this, I tell people to think of a marriage or any long-term relationship in which two people have gotten to know each other very well. You say, "What's wrong?" Your spouse replies, "Nothing." Yet because of the way he or she looks or sits or talks, you know that person is upset or excited or nervous. But how long has it taken you to pick up on those little cues? A customer or client, whom you meet once, maybe a few more times, is not going to be aware of these things. That's why communicating to your client like this seems to be magic—the communication is real, but on a very deep level.

Selling to Groups

When you are making a presentation to a group of people, be aware that you should still sell to them individually, not just as a group. Since walking into a roomful of people doesn't give me the chance to find out everybody's favorite mode of thinking so easily, I make sure I use all three modes throughout my presentation. I always try to illustrate my points with whatever visual material is most appropriate: slides, videotapes, brochures, and drawings. I try to tickle their ears with some alliterations and word play. For example, instead of saying, "Even those fools who think they're above it all will go for this," I like to say, "Even a sharp college boy like me who was senior class president *twice* will go for this." Another favorite, when I'm referring to difficult economic times: "Even those who never intended to pay aren't buying."

To build rapport with the kinesthetics in the group, I try to sprinkle my presentation with physical participation: I ask them to raise their hands in answer to certain questions. To emphasize a point, I ask them to touch or tap the person next to them. Even writing out something works well, because it gets them to do something physical.

If someone in the group asks me to clarify something, for example, "I don't know if I understand this," I try to answer by saying: "Here's the way it should look," then, "Does this sound good so far?" and "If anyone can't get a handle on what I'm saying, please raise your hand." By going from one mode to the next during the course of my presentation, I keep everyone involved at all times. I am also performing that important function: checking to ascertain that everyone is still with me.

Slides are always a good visual selling tool for multiple clients. You can use slides to great effect even if you are selling to only two or three people. Just be careful not to darken the room too much, which could cause your clients to fall asleep. I find that a happy medium works best. The room is light enough so that clients aren't lulled into the sense of isolation that darkness brings, yet dark enough to bring out the colors and shapes of slides or transparencies.

When using slides, avoid using black and white. Black is significantly associated with death and dying. White is very hard to see, and will make adjusting the lights that much more difficult. And it's very important to make sure that you turn the projector off before switching transparencies. You want to avoid letting your clients be forced to look at the projector's bright light when there is no transparency in it.

It takes patience and a little practice, but once you are used to picking up on cues, communicating in a customer's preferred mode becomes second nature. Always remember: Read your customer's cues, keep checking yourself throughout your presentation, and switch modes if you have to. When you are comfortable doing these things, you are ready to learn even more sophisticated and powerful techniques of building rapport and selling to your customers.

PART II

CREATING MAGIC: TECHNIQUES FOR A SUCCESSFUL SALES STRATEGY

NeuroLinguistic Programming is based on the belief in options. A successful general has more than one strategy. A football team with the greater number of plays and the capability of carrying them out can prevail over a team with more talent. The same holds true for the salesperson: The more ways you have of communicating trust to that unique person across the desk, the more successful you will be.

We discussed the importance of communicating in your client's preferred mode of thinking in the first part of the book. Use this knowledge as a foundation for the techniques you will learn in Part Two. The techniques can be applied whether or not you are aware if someone is a visual, auditory, or kinesthetic. But if you learn to use these techniques while communicating in your client's preferred mode, you will have very powerful selling tools at your disposal. Throughout this second section, you will see how the combination of the two makes for a much more sophisticated and effective way of gaining rapport and earning trust.

The selling techniques described in the following chapters will teach you to work directly with your client's unconscious. If you master them, I promise that you will develop the competence the supersellers have. You will read what's below the surface, and sell based on what your client is communicating to you at a deeper level. You will ask more probing questions, present your ideas more forcefully, and close successfully—because you will be aware of what your client is really thinking and feeling.

In the first three chapters of this section, I'll share some insights about listening, as well as verbal and physical techniques that will greatly reinforce rapport with your client and create new selling opportunities for you. Then you will discover how to let your clients do some of your selling for you: *By asking the right questions, you'll get them to tell you what they really want to buy, even if they initially say they don't know.* You will also learn about pacing your meeting—how to speed up or slow down your presentation as needed, depending on the feedback you are getting. And you will learn how to bring your client effortlessly to the very point of buying by expertly dealing with objections and closing a sale at the right time.

Someone once said that a sale merely consummates the courtship. I couldn't agree more. For those of us who love selling, it is the process that matters. I love the challenge of searching for the solution to a client's needs, presenting it effectively, and seeing my client's face light up when he or she says, "Yes, let's do it." Making the actual sale is always important, but it is in getting my clients to that point that I get the most satisfaction from my work. After becoming acquainted with these techniques, I hope you will feel the same way.

A smart salesperson listens to emotions, not facts.

CHAPTER THREE

Effective Listening: The Bottom Line of Trust

Much has been written about the importance of listening astutely in business. Mark McCormack, the well-known manager of celebrity sports figures and author of *What They Don't Teach You at Harvard Business School*, says, "In selling, there is probably no greater asset." He also notes that when he asked a number of other business leaders what they considered important for business success, most of them came up with *listening*.

You can't establish trust if you can't listen. A conversation is a relationship. Both speaker and listener play a part, each influencing the other. Instead of merely being a passive recipient, the listener has as much to do in shaping the conversation as the speaker. The magic of successful entrepreneurs like Mark McCormack and others who have made it to the top is that they've learned how to use this process to create business opportunities for themselves.

People have commented on what a good listener I am. I used to think this was a weakness. I've often thought that by keeping my ideas and views to myself too often, people would not be as interested in me. But I've found that they usually care more about what they have to say than what I might be telling them. Clients like to feel that they are important to you; remember, you are there to meet their needs, not the other way around.

In sales, the person doing the talking is perceived to be the one controlling the conversation. Just the opposite is true. If you really listen, you have a lot of influence on the conversation. Effective listening involves work on your part. It is more a mental activity than a physical one. You take in what your customer is saying to you and then use that information to make the best sale you can.

A smart salesperson listens to emotions, not facts. I often use the image of an iceberg in describing communication. Only about 20 percent of an iceberg is visible; 80 percent is below the surface. When you listen to facts, you are hearing only 20 percent of what someone is communicating to you. When you listen to emotions, you are paying attention to the other 80 percent.

You ask Mrs. Jones how she likes a certain product, for example. She says, "Fine. It's great." But her voice is flat and she sounds somewhat bored. If you are paying attention to what's below the surface, you know that something isn't fine. You can then use that information to probe further.

Unfortunately, most of us don't listen. We keep talking and talking to the point that we actually oversell. This becomes a problem, because most of the time, we sell right past the point that a client is willing to buy. By talking too much, we buy the product right back.

Have you ever talked to someone who looked at other people walking by as you spoke? Didn't you feel like slapping this person a couple of times and saying, "Pay attention"? To impress upon other salespeople how important the feeling of being listened to is, I like to tell the story of my three-year-old daughter. I sometimes try to do work while she sits nearby, asking me a dozen questions, as only a toddler can. I respond like a good dutiful father with "That's nice, sweetheart . . . great . . . Oh boy!" After a few minutes of this she usually gets exasperated, gets up on my lap, grabs my face, and demands, "Did you hear me,

Daddy?'' With my lips protruding like those of a puffer fish, I say, "Yes, honey. I'm really listening now!''

Your clients may not physically grab you like a toddler might, but believe me, they would like to. Sometimes knowing that you're really listening is all it takes to turn a client around. I was trying to sell my services to an executive of a large manufacturer of home appliances. A trade convention was coming up to be attended by a lot of independent distributors who sold this manufacturer's products. I tried to get the executive to hire me as a speaker to give this audience some tips on selling. Since these distributors weren't direct employees of the manufacturer, I knew they would appreciate this added bonus. Their loyalty to the manufacturer and its products would increase.

As I stood there talking with this manufacturer, probing him with questions, he threw up some very serious objections. One was simply that my speaking fee was too high. He kept saying how high-priced I was, and that he couldn't afford my fee.

I was tempted to interrupt him and show him how much value he would receive by hiring me—value in the form of distributor loyalty, which would help his company in the long run. That concept, in which results aren't readily apparent, is the hardest thing to sell. As we were going back and forth, I realized the best way to handle the situation was to keep quiet and let him do the talking. After about a minute, I was astounded to hear him overcome his own objection.

"But then again, I guess it would increase our corporate sales overall," he suddenly said. "I also think that the distributors' salespeople need information like this. It will increase our sales as well as their own. Oh, let's go ahead with it.''

If I had interrupted him at any step during that interview process, I would have oversold. Instead of buying the product back, however, I kept quiet and let him state what we both knew was true all along.

Listening well isn't easy. We think (that is, listen) ten to twelve times faster than we talk. Concentrating on what someone is telling us instead of racing ahead or thinking about something else takes effort. Here is an exercise for you to try with a friend or relative. Listen to a story or problem he or she wants to tell you, but refrain from giving any feedback. How do you feel about keeping quiet? What reactions do you get from the speaker? How long can you continue listening before you have to say something?

The answers to these questions are a good indication of your feelings about listening. Some people realize they feel threatened when put in this position. They have a need to talk instead. If you have this need, you are giving up control of the conversation, because you are not focused on the speaker. Other people find that they can't concentrate at all when they're not allowed to give feedback. Their attention drifts. This too represents a loss of control, because such people can't process what they're hearing.

Always keep in mind that you can't fake listening. If you pretend, your clients will pick up on it. I like the way superbroker Richard F. Greene of Merrill Lynch in Boston thinks of it. In an interview with *Fortune* magazine, he said he doesn't go to a meeting to sell a prospective client. He goes to listen. "If I do the talking, my business will not be served. Now this fellow [the client] is the same as everyone else. His kids don't listen to him. His wife doesn't listen to him—and he doesn't listen to her. When he goes to parties the person he's talking to is looking over his shoulder to see what else is going on in the room. Then all of a sudden he goes to breakfast with me. He starts to answer a question. And he doesn't get interrupted."

The father of interpersonal psychology, Carl Rogers once wrote of good listening, "We can't use it as a technique until we demonstrate a spirit which genuinely respects the potential worth of the individual." Your clients want you to show them that respect. Rogers was talking about therapy. I've discovered that it's just as important and productive in sales.

The Eight Steps of Active Listening

The eight steps listed below will make you an active participant in the listening process. Besides reinforcing rapport, which is always your goal, listening actively to your customers or clients will get them to open themselves up more easily, listen to your ideas, and be less defensive. Integrating these steps into the way you listen will help you diffuse hostility and make your clients feel more relaxed and comfortable. When they feel this way, they will present you with selling opportunities on their own.

1. Value the speaker. Your customer may not be as articulate as you are. Or you may know what your client is going to say in a given situation. It doesn't matter. You always need to show concern and demonstrate that you respect the position your speaker is in.

When I was first trying to sell my services as a motivational speaker, I used to feel impatient with the resistance I would meet. The people responsible for booking speakers, like the executive of the home-appliance manufacturer mentioned earlier, often seemed to have no idea of the benefits they could gain from hiring someone like me. The excuses they kept giving me for not using my services never did make sense when looked at more closely, yet I had a hard time convincing them differently.

In thinking about why I was successful with the executive in the earlier example, I realized I was more patient with him—I respected who he was and what he was trying to do. This man had previously been a salesman and had built up his own business just as I had done. Now he was back in corporate life. And though now he was saying almost exactly the same things I heard over and over, I put more value in him because of his previous experience. I was more willing to listen and let his concerns play themselves out—and because of that, I gained a sale. I didn't have to *do* anything—it was my attitude that made the difference.

2. *Listen to what is not said.* Another way of saying this is: Pay attention to the 80 percent of the iceberg that's underwater.

Deletions and distortions are part of everything we say. They make up the hidden 80 percent of any conversation. If you train yourself to "listen between the lines," you will be able to really hear what someone is telling you. And you'll be able to use that information to ask more probing questions without making your client feel overly challenged.

To give you a few examples, what does your client mean when he says, "I can't use this product"? Is he saying he doesn't know how to use it, he doesn't want to use it, he has another product in mind? What is he leaving out of this statement? Instead of challenging him directly, try to find out more specifics. What is it about this product that makes it useless? How would he like it changed? Does he have a substitute in mind?

How about the following statement from someone representing an entire company: "We have found such systems don't work very well." Who is "we"? Certain departments or employees, or the company as a whole? His statement seems overly generalized. There is also a comparison implied here. What *does* work well? Is there something that worked better in the past?

In asking prospective clients to expand on their statements, it's very important not to challenge them directly. That would break rapport. Instead, by focusing on what's not said, you can ask questions that don't contradict anything your clients have already told you. It's a way of getting them to open up further without making them feel as though you are forcing them to do it.

Sometimes there is a fine line between what you perceive as nonchallenging and how your prospective customer looks at it. In the winter of 1993, I was doing a lot of speaking in Europe and was referred to a consultant for a life insurance association in Ireland. When he called me to find out whether I would be able to speak at the association's annual conference, he asked me typical information: my fee, my background, how long I might speak, and what I would say. By the end of the conversation, he seemed excited about me and asked me to hold the date open until he could consult with his program committee.

Not having heard from him for about a month, I finally called him while speaking in London. This time, he seemed far less enthusiastic, even abrupt, informing me he had already booked all the speakers for the conference. "I'm a little confused," I told him. "What happened in the past month? When we talked, the schedule was fully open."

"You're kind of a pushy American, aren't you?" he replied. I felt insulted. If something doesn't work out, I always try to find out why. Trying to sound as polite as possible, I told the meeting planner as much, asking him if I waited too long to call, or whether it was something else that made me lose the booking.

After a few moments of embarrassed silence, the planner admitted that they had no budget for a speaker like me. He told me that one of their suppliers was speaking for free.

If I had not asked him a "pushy" question, I would have thought I hadn't presented myself well enough. As it turned out, this situation had nothing to do with me. He was embarrassed to admit that he had misrepresented the organization. This kind of distortion of the truth happens to me all the time—on both sides of the Atlantic. People come up to me at conferences, talk up their organization, promise to use me at upcoming meetings, and then I find out they aren't authorized to do anything of the sort, or the organization doesn't have any money, or isn't big enough to use outside speakers.

It is critical that you listen between the lines. Clients have a lot of reasons for being evasive or simply dishonest. You deserve to know the truth, even at the risk of appearing slightly pushy. Hone your listening skills so that you catch anything that doesn't make sense, and ask follow-up questions until you're satisfied that you know what the real story is.

3. *Try to hear the truth.* Sometimes what your clients say

is true, but you don't want to listen. They may give you objections or tell you things that you don't want to hear about your product, or even about your sales ability. If some of these comments sound rude or threaten to undermine preconceived ideas you have about yourself, you will be doubly resentful.

Put those preconceived ideas aside. Concentrate on the truth of the comments, instead of who is saying them.

A manager of a very large company currently says to his marketing staff, "Forget who said it. Is there truth to it?" He started this campaign because his staff members were very quick to find excuses when they received criticism from customers. "Well, this guy's just a crank anyway," they would say. "What does he know?" or "This woman doesn't even pay her bills on time. Why should we listen to her?"

The fact of the matter is, even if your client is confused, inarticulate, or even rude, there might be some truth to what he or she is saying. Forget who is speaking and listen instead to the truth of their comments.

4. *Limit the time you speak.* Research has shown that prospective customers have an attention span that lasts about thirty seconds. There has been much talk lately about how short our attention spans are getting. Television advertisers have known for a long time that if their ads last for more than thirty seconds each, you will go get a cup of coffee, a snack, or change the channel. In fact, most television producers know that if they keep a camera shot during a TV program on one place for more than 4.5 seconds, viewer interest will dissipate.

As a rule, make sure that you never talk for more than thirty seconds at a time without asking, "Any comments about this?" "Any questions?" Asking your client what he or she thinks is a good way to reinforce rapport and ensure that a person's attention does not wander. Thirty seconds really is a long time. Try timing yourself while talking sometime. You will be surprised how long thirty seconds really is.

Remember to treat people the way *they* want to be treated. When your clients are doing the talking, don't interrupt. You will be able to control the interview more effectively by letting your clients talk until they have communicated to their satisfaction, not yours. As I stressed in the beginning of the chapter, it is often more important for your clients to hear themselves tell you their problems than it is for them to hear what you say. If they think you are listening, they will be much more motivated to buy from you.

5. *Avoid the tendency to think about what you will say after your customers stop talking.* A good salesperson is sharp enough to be spontaneous, not canned. You shouldn't try to manipulate customers by asking certain questions that you already know the answers to.

If you think about what you want to say while your customers are talking, you will certainly miss their message. When you miss even the smallest part of what someone is saying, you may miss the information that will generate a sale for you.

Listen intently to your customer's answer to a question or comment before you speak. Then answer appropriately.

6. *Listen to your customer's point of view.* We have an adage in sales that goes something like this: Everybody buys from someone sometime. If a prospect doesn't buy from you, he will buy from someone else who better understands his needs and solves his problems.

Even though you may think you understand the concerns of your customers, always keep in mind that this person has a unique perception of the world. Try to understand this point of view by concentrating on the process in which your customer says things and by paying attention to the thoughts behind the words. Listen for meaning and intent behind the actual content.

Practically every salesman has heard at least once in his career, "Yes, I know your product is wonderful and that you're selling it at a good price, but I don't need it."

And every salesman has wanted or tried to say, "But if you'll only let me explain it to you, you would see how it can help you."

In the above exchange, the client is really saying, "Fulfill my needs." The salesman is really saying, "I can sell you if you listen to me talk."

Such an exchange has a great deal to do with perceptions. Whether it is true or not, the customer certainly believes that he doesn't need that product. And the salesperson sincerely believes that the product would be beneficial to the customer.

In the chapter about outcomes, you will learn how to get beyond this point and find out why your client is resisting you. The important point here is that you have to keep an open mind and credit each perspective as being valid. When you are listening to your customer, don't listen critically or analytically. Just listen to see how that person thinks. Tell yourself, That's valid from that person's vantage point.

7. *Repeat your clients' comments to make sure they know you heard what they said.* I write monthly for over fifteen magazines from coast to coast. Frequently, I don't have time to write fifteen different articles. Instead, I agree to have some articles repeated, trying to give exclusivity to magazines in specific industries.

I was speaking to one of my editors and thought I heard her tell me that she wanted my articles to appear in her magazines only, nowhere else. This was extremely difficult because of my time constraints. I knew that if I agreed to what she was asking, I would spend all my time writing.

When I repeated back to her what I thought she said, I was shocked to find out that she didn't mean that at all. She merely meant that she didn't want three of her most competitive magazines to have my articles. That was no problem. By repeating what I had heard, I saved myself a lot of extra work.

8. *Don't take extensive notes while listening.* Extensive note-taking breaks rapport with the speaker. It becomes very distracting, because your speaker will be on to a new thought before you have finished writing down the previous one. You will spend more energy reestablishing rapport and trying to catch up with your speaker than actually listening.

Instead, jot down an occasional key word or phrase that will help you recall the conversation later on. This actually reinforces rapport, because your speaker realizes that you are interested in what he is saying.

As a listener, don't forget the importance of eye contact. From our discussion of preferred modes of thinking, you may think that only visuals care about eye contact. That is untrue. Auditories and kinesthetics may not consciously worry about eye contact—they may not notice the color of your eyes while talking with you or later remember whether you broke eye contact—but they are affected by it, too. Remember, we are talking about preferred modes of thinking, not exclusive ones. Depending on the situation, your clients may switch from one mode to another. Just as you don't take chances by being polite only to people who are polite to you, you don't take chances with eye contact.

Maintaining eye contact tells your clients that you are in rapport with them. Make sure that you don't stare your clients down, but offer a sincere look that communicates interest and caring. If I sense that my client looks away or seems uncomfortable with something, I look away as well for a few seconds. This builds rapport because it gives clients time to readjust and refocus their thoughts.

Reflective and Paraphrase Listening

Reflective listening is simply repeating some words your clients use as you listen to them speak. Someone says, "I read your book last year and I liked it." You respond, "You read my book?" perhaps with a slight nod, and continue listening. Or, a customer says, "I had a BMW last year and I didn't like it—it drove kind of rough." "It drove kind of rough, huh," you respond and leave it at that, letting the customer continue speaking.

Reflective listening deepens rapport three ways: It shows that you are paying attention; that you understand what the person is telling you; and that you care. It is a great way to keep someone talking and revealing more of what he might want from you or a product.

Many times customers need to work off some steam—complaining about what's happening at their company, talking about the high price of doing business, venting dissatisfaction with products—before they are ready to really talk with you. Reflective listening is a way to keep rapport developing while you're waiting to get down to the real issues.

A securities salesman whom I knew professionally called me once asking if we could get together. This man had been in the business for twenty years, and was routinely making a million or two a year in commissions. Suddenly, at the age of forty-four, he found himself losing motivation. His income was dropping, he was thinking about becoming an actor, opening up a restaurant—he wasn't sure himself what he wanted.

As we sat down to talk, I started giving him some advice. He interrupted me, brushing aside all my comments. I finally settled in and listened for two hours, repeating a word and comment here and there. Finally, in the last ten minutes, he was ready to listen to my advice. I certainly can't claim I solved his life's problems, but the point is, I couldn't tell him anything until he was ready to hear it.

While I know that I can't waste an entire day listening to a client's problems, I've also learned that a certain amount of listening is a good investment. Sometimes, if the stakes are high enough, I'm willing to invest a lot of hours and any number of meetings. Listening reflectively makes it a little easier on me emotionally. The client has my attention and knows it, yet the work required to give that attention is minimal.

Paraphrase listening works on a similar principle, except that you paraphrase what your client has just said. If someone tells you, for example, "The maintenance on your copiers is going through the roof," you can say, "Yes, servicing copy machines is a very expensive proposition."

Use both active and reflective listening to enhance rapport and to keep yourself on your toes. It will help keep your clients talking until they are really ready to get down to business.

Shared Listening

Have you ever had a salesperson ask you a million questions, making you feel that you were on the receiving end of a machine gun? "What kind of car do you drive now? How long have you had it? What's its mileage? Any problems with the engine? How's the body holding up?"

No one likes to be sold that way, yet a lot of salespeople have been trained to ask questions as a way of finding out information. Shared listening takes you out of this survey mode. You turn listening into a conversation so that your clients don't feel as if they're being interrogated.

Here's how it works:

Kerry:	What kind of car do you drive now?
Customer:	A Subaru.
Kerry:	Any problems?
Customer:	Well, I've had some trouble with the exhaust system, but other than that it's OK.
Kerry:	You're not alone. My wife had two Subarus—decent cars, but they both needed exhaust work after about sixty thousand miles. I also didn't think the engine was that powerful.
Customer:	Sounds like *my* car. Not much pickup at

	all. But let me tell you something, I'd rather have that and great mileage.
Kerry:	Oh? We get about twenty-five miles per gallon.
Customer:	I'm getting almost thirty.

Developing a conversation, rather than asking one question after another, is a great way to get a person to open up. I use this technique when someone seems reluctant to talk for whatever reason. When I share some of my own feelings about a product, it makes clients more comfortable and leads them to other ideas. If I can share feelings in the same mode of thought, my client feels even more comfortable. In the above example, the customer uses some auditory predicates: *sounds*; *let me tell you*. As you continue the conversation, you would want to use auditory predicates of your own. This would make the customer respond even further, giving you a lot of information that you can later use in the selling process.

I once spoke at a regional symposium of financial planners. A gentleman who owns a bank management consulting company was also a featured speaker at this symposium. After his presentation, I saw him at a restaurant and had a cup of coffee with him. I spent most of my time listening while he told me about his expertise in approaching banks and showing them how they could make more money by underwriting certain bonds.

While he was talking, I listened intently and repeated some of his words. We "spoke" for about an hour and a half, and I said almost nothing except for reinforcement of his comments.

A month later, he called me up and said he was the program chairman for the Young Presidents' Organization—an enormously powerful group of men and women aged forty-nine and under who own their own businesses. This man said he wanted me to speak at one of their upcoming conventions. When I asked him why he had picked me, he told me that I was very wise and articulate and that many of the Young Presidents' members could learn a lot from me.

This invitation was particularly curious to me, since he had found out very little about me during our restaurant conversation. Yet, we had developed a strong bond simply because I had listened to him so intently.

Never underestimate the power of listening. The very fact that someone knows you are really listening produces trust. If you're not afraid to let go of your need to sell to your client and just pay attention to what's being said to you, you'll be surprised how much easier the process becomes.

If someone uses words that hold special meaning for you, more than just information is conveyed. You instinctively feel that you've been understood.

CHAPTER FOUR

Verbal Techniques That Build Trust

In the previous chapter, I discussed reflective and paraphrase listening, which involves repeating a client's words and phrases to deepen rapport and keep information flowing. You can take word repetition to a more sophisticated level by repeating words that you know hold special meaning for a client. Knowing how to distinguish such words and then using them back to a client is one of the verbal strategies you will learn in this chapter.

There are more than three hundred thousand words in an unabridged English dictionary. We use only about 1 percent in ordinary speech, and a select few of that percentage take on special meaning for us. This special meaning comes from the emotions that lie behind everything we say. We all have our own unique history. Somewhere in the past, we associated certain terms with a particular emotion, and that association has stuck. Such words may be very ordinary and carry no extra meaning for anyone else, but to us, they're important. The one who can pick up on such words and use them back to you is doing more than just conveying information. That person makes you instinctively feel that you've been understood.

Using Key Words

William Gates is the chairman of Microsoft, the world's largest supplier of personal computer software. Named the richest man in America by *Forbes* magazine in the fall of 1992 (he is now worth about seven *billion* dollars), he has been getting a lot of attention recently. In reading accounts of how he is coping with his success, I was struck by how much key words can express someone's real feelings.

Although his primary duties now consist of marketing and business decisions in running Microsoft, Gates spends a lot of time in laboratories and with programmers, going over details of new software. Those who interview him remark on how he peppers his speech with technical terms related to programming, such as *bandwidth*, *random*, *hardcore*. These words are not just a game to Gates. By using them constantly he is showing how important that "techie" side of him still is. Even though Microsoft is a big company and he is now a wealthy CEO, he seems to be saying over and over how comfortable he is with the technical side of things, and how important it is for him to stay involved in it.

Those who use such words back to him are the ones who have an edge in getting hired. If you were selling something to this man, that edge could mean a difference in terms of millions of dollars.

Key words can be jargon, as in the case of Bill Gates. Jargon often carries a lot of emotional weight. Every profession and industry has its special terms, signifying that the person using them is an insider. If you can meaningfully use the jargon in your presentation back to a client, do it. It's a great rapport builder.

Key words are also those words that pop out at you because they're colorful or extreme in meaning. If you're selling a house and your client says, "What I want is an incredible view," you know your client means really wonderful, not just good or adequate. And when you show your client the house, you reinforce the idea by saying, "Tom, here's that house you and I talked about. I think you'll agree that you're looking at an incredible view right now."

Using people's key words or phrases makes them more receptive to you, because they feel you've been receptive to them. One of my key phrases is "like a cheap suit." I use it often to refer to something that a person is attracted to. I was making a video for one of my training sessions recently, and the producer asked me why I used a particular example. I told him if I use it, "People will be on me like a cheap suit." The phrase must have popped out at him, because during the course of making the video I asked him if we had to use so many special effects. He retorted, "Yes. If you do, your viewers will be on you like a cheap suit."

Remember that when you hear a key word, you do some further probing to find out exactly what associations the word or phrase has for your client. If you were the realtor in the first example, you would ask what *incredible* means to your client. Just the fact that you have picked up on the importance of the word and are asking further questions related to it tells your client that you have really listened to him.

It is also important to be flexible and adopt key words or phrases that at first might seem strange or taken out of context. A life insurance agent recently told me a story about a meeting he had with a woman who wanted advice on financial planning. At one point he heard her say that she wanted protection with "an increase in income as an investment." These were not the words that the agent had learned to associate with the insurance he sold. He was accustomed to saying, "security with high protection."

Applying my ideas to his presentations, he told her: "I understand that you want protection with an increase in income. Here's how this product will help you . . . . Does this look OK?" He didn't try to change her way of describing what she wanted. He was flexible, reusing the words that were meaningful to her.

Don't forget how you can apply your knowledge of mental maps in conjunction with using key words. Suppose the woman had said, "What sounds best to me is increase in income as an investment," and had used other auditory predicates during her speech. The agent could have said, "I hear what you're saying—you want protection with an increase in income. Here's how this product will help you . . . . Does this sound OK?"

I hope you are beginning to appreciate the power of unconscious competence. The salesman could increase rapport not only with *what* he said to her, but in *how* he said it. Her trust in his ability to provide the product she wanted would go up dramatically.

Because they feel strongly about the merits of their product, many salespeople try to change a customer's vocabulary. Don't. Add to it, instead. Although I'm often billed as one, I hate the term motivational speaker. To me it implies something rather superficial and quick fix, an Elmer Gantry you-are-healed approach to things. If clients and audiences are fired up and motivated after listening to me, that's wonderful. But I prefer to bill myself as an author, speaker, and sales psychologist.

Unfortunately, the market for sales psychologists doesn't seem as identifiable as the one for motivational speakers. I often feel like the washing-machine salesman who wants to call his latest model a four-cycle clothes recompressor. To the average customer, however, it's still basically a washing machine. In my case, the term motivational speaker is so prevalent, I just smile and use the label too, building on it by explaining how I work.

Jot down key phrases as clients talk with you. Then, when the time comes, you can match those words as you sum up and close your presentation. I once called a vice president of a stock brokerage firm on a referral. I listened well and talked with him for about twenty minutes. As we said good-bye, he signed off with this phrase: "Whatever you do, do it well. Have fun and do plenty of it." Guess how I signed off on a letter that I later sent to him? I picked up on one of the easiest sales I ever made.

Marking Out

Just as we use punctuation to give emphasis and clarity to our writing, we use verbal cues to punctuate what we say. Most people slow the pace of their speech when they use words that hold special meaning, pausing right before and after the word. They punch the word up, and the tone of their voice can also change, either going up or down. This verbal way of punching up speech is called marking out.

Learning to distinguish marked-out words and using them back to a client gives you an even more subtle way of reinforcing rapport. Here's an example:

Kerry: I fly eight thousand miles a week on speaking engagements.

Friend: Gee, that's a lot of traveling.

Kerry: Yes, I love speaking, but I . . . hate . . . traveling.

I used to have this exchange a lot and never did much to change my schedule. Lately, I have begun to notice how much I emphasize the word *hate* by pausing and letting my voice drop when I use it. Coincidentally, this comes at a time when I've decided to stop extensive traveling and write this book. What I'm telling myself and my listener by marking out *hate* is that it is a word full of impact for me. Someone trying to sell me something that involved a lot of travel would be wise to stay away.

Marking out is most useful with ordinary words, words that you would pass right over if it weren't for that pause or change of tone. It is the way such words are said, rather than their meaning, that clues you in to their importance. Sometimes, marking out is accompanied by body language such as finger pointing or a movement of the hands. Or, your customer may look up or look away to mark out a word. You may not know what a person really means by marking out such a word, but you'll sense something is up when the word is used.

When you think you've noticed a marked-out word, keep it in mind and then use it back to your customer at an appropriate time. Watch for a response. If you sense that you've hit on something important, you can go further and build some of your presentation around it.

A prospective client once told me, "Whoever I pick as a speaker has to be fair about travel expenses." He paused before the word *fair* and punched it up.

It would have been easy to let the comment pass, thinking, *Well, that's ridiculous. I'm always fair.* But I asked him, "What does *fair* mean to you?" He replied, "Flying coach, not first class." He was referring to the fact that most speakers fly first class.

Because I didn't let the comment go, I picked up on something that might have seemed insignificant to me, but was very important to the speaker. As he has subsequently told me, he has hired (and rehired) me because I'm the only fair speaker he has seen.

Even if you aren't sure that a word or term is important but suspect that it is, ask about it. An editor friend of mine was having a job interview (and what is an interview but a selling of your services?), during which his prospective employer said, "I want a hands-on editor." This is a fairly common term that refers to an editor who works on the nuts and bolts of a manuscript, rather than one who spends more time signing up authors and looking out for new projects. When he first heard the term, my friend let it pass, knowing that he always worked very hard on editing and reediting every manuscript. But his prospective employer repeated it a second time, and it dawned on my friend to ask him what the employer meant by the term. It turned out that he had had some bad experiences with editors who were more concerned with the acquisitions part of editing, and he did not want to repeat the same mistake. By stopping and discussing the problem at length, my friend was able to reassure his prospective employer that that would not be the case with him, and he got the job.

The Fifteen Most Persuasive Words

As you may have guessed, there are certain key words that appeal to practically every American. These key words are utilized by television, radio, and print advertisers with enormous effectiveness. Some of these words are so effective, that even though companies overuse them, people still respond to them positively.

Advertisers have been light-years ahead of the rest of us in appreciating how certain words have great psychological impact. They understand that words can motivate, bring back memories, evoke deep feelings. They know how to use words to persuade, entice, cajole, entertain, and in the best of circumstances, educate. They've learned how words can make people look at things in totally new ways and perhaps try something they have never tried before.

Even with all the quick-cut visuals and computer-generated graphics we see in advertising nowadays, words and slogans are still very much a part of the game. Nuprin's "Nupe it," Express Mail's "We Deliver for You," Bose Music Systems' "M.I.T. Meets Mozart," and the slogan for McDonald's, "What You Want Is What You Get," appeal very strongly to our auditory sense and fulfill unspoken desires. And how about the old slogans that are still being used because they bring back such fond memories: "Have You Driven a Ford Lately?"; Campbell's soups' "M'm! M'm! Good!"; and Clairol's "Does She or Doesn't She?"

Advertisers know that by using words and slogans with their products, they are getting the attention of potential customers on different levels: auditorially with the word play itself, and kinesthetically because of the different feelings the words evoke.

(My favorite kinesthetic slogan of recent years comes from Toyota: "It's not how many touches a car has, it's how it touches you.") When these slogans are coupled with the images we see on television or in print, we are being appealed to in all three modes of perception.

I've put together a list of words both from research studies and from what I've seen advertisers use over and over. Year in and year out, these words find new audiences or retain old ones. Remember them when you sell. Use them in your presentations, on the telephone, and in written correspondence when you follow up with your client. These universal key words will evoke the same feelings toward your product that advertisers have been evoking so expertly for decades.

1. Discover. In the 1980s, Sears Financial Services came out with the first credit card to seriously challenge the dominance of American Express, Visa, and MasterCard. It was called the Discover card.

Sears put a lot of money into researching the name of the card. They didn't just pick the name out of thin air. They had to choose a word that would generate interest, evoke a feeling of opportunity, and suggest a better life. Remember that when you tell your clients that they will discover something, you will evoke the same feeling.

2. Good. "As good as mother used to make"; "It's good for you"; "The Good Olds Guys." *Good* is not a high-powered word, and that is the secret of its success. It evokes stability and security. If something is good for your clients, they will want to buy it. And by extension, if it's good, it's not bad. Everyone wants to be associated with what's good.

3. Money. Few people feel they have enough, and everybody wants more.

4. Easy. What everyone wants is more simplicity and the ability to do things more easily. If your product can make something easier for would-be purchasers, they will be more apt to buy it.

5. *Guaranteed.* One of the fears most human beings have is taking a risk. They want to know that if your product doesn't work out, they can get their money back.

6. *Health.* Remember the expression, "If I've got my health, I've got everything"? If a product promotes financial, emotional, or physical health, it offers a big plus. To many people, this is even more important than money.

7. *Love.* Many companies make enormous amounts of money selling love. Whether it's dating services or vacations for single people, love is always a prime selling hook. Leo Buscaglia and John Bradshaw have become best-selling authors by writing about love and how it should be shared.

8. *New.* If it's new, it must be better. It's a tried-and-true concept that seems to be part of the American mystique. And although there is always the occasional fiasco, like the New Coke debacle of a few years' back, we still like to think of ourselves as being on the cutting edge. Just think back to Bill Clinton's inauguration speech in 1993. He talked about renewal and change. Unless a product is specifically targeted to evoke nostalgia, with images of Mom or apple pie, anyone who tries to sell something old-fashioned meets with limited success.

9. *Proven.* Although we like new things, we want reliability as well. We want something that has been tested and proven not to be harmful in any way. We also don't want something that will break down or require a lot of servicing. We don't want to doubt that something will work.

10. *Results.* Another twist to the American psyche. Although we may mouth the words, underneath we don't care about trying hard and putting forth our best efforts if we don't see results. We want to know exactly what we're getting for spending our money.

11. *Safe.* This closely parallels health. We all value our lives, and if a product is safe, or our assets are safe, we are much more trusting.

12. *Save.* Saving money is almost as important as making

money. If a company can't promise that you will make money with a product, it usually promises to help you save money. Saving is better than spending. A recent ad for Buick said it best: "Just because you've earned it doesn't mean you have to spend it."

13. Own. We all like to own things. Owning is better than buying, because it implies possession rather than more spending. When you present a product, talk about owning it rather than buying it.

14. Free. We love to say you can't get something for nothing, but we don't believe it. Just think of all the mail solicitations you receive with the word *FREE* emblazoned on the envelope. Or all the times you see the word in print or television advertising. "Free" is an instant eye catcher, something that compels you to look further. If you can use *free* in any selling that you do, pointing out that your customer will get something for nothing, use it. You'll get your customer's attention immediately.

15. Best. If you know that a product has been shown to be the best in any way, shape, or form, be sure your customer is made aware of it. Possessing something that has been shown to be the best in mileage, has the best service record, has won a taste test exerts a very powerful pull to have it for ourselves.

Reframing

Reframing is taking a negative or neutral situation and turning it around into something more positive and useful. The 3M company was having trouble with one of its adhesive products—it didn't seem strong enough. One of the company's research and development people put a bit of the adhesive on the back of a small piece of paper. The lightweight adhesive allowed the paper scrap to be stuck on and taken off, and Post-its were born. The researcher had reframed the troublesome adhesive into a product that has made millions.

You can do the same thing in selling, using a situation where rapport is superficial or nonexistent and taking it to a deeper, more complex level. Think of the standard greetings you give to someone: "How are you?" "How's it going?" The use of these phrases is almost automatic in our society. They don't show much thought or caring. When was the last time you said, "How are you?" and someone actually told you truthfully how he or she felt? Even if you ask people who are noticeably ill, as with the flu, how they are, they will usually say, "Fine, thanks." It's a quick, automatic response to a standard question.

The next time you see a client, try reframing your greeting. Instead of "How are you?" say something like, "How is your day going?" It's the same question, but you are literally forcing him out of an automatic response, to actually think about your question. Or you can ask, "Has your day been productive?" "Are things going smoothly for you?" If you reframe your greeting in this way, your clients won't be able to pass it off as a meaningless remark. When they have to think about what you've said, it translates into caring, which translates into greater rapport and trust.

Like a picture frame that can change the impact of a painting, you can reframe any concept or situation. Think of reframing as relabeling. Insurance agents around the United States have been reframing their titles. Many have started to call themselves "Financial Services Advisor," or "Financial Consultant." By doing so, they undercut many of the negative ideas their clients have about insurance salesmen. A client's response to an insurance salesman is often, "I don't need any insurance." On the other hand, most would like help with their finances, as well as budgeting and investing.

Mary Kay Cosmetics has done a great job in reframing their salespeople. Instead of calling them simply "cosmetics salespersons," they now refer to their reps as Mary Kay Consultants. *Consultant* conveys the idea that this person will help solve problems. In the case of Mary Kay Cosmetics, one thinks of someone who will help women look better and help them answer questions they may have about many things related to makeup.

One salesman I know who was working in Neiman Marcus decided that he was going to reframe himself. When customers asked what he did for a living, he told them that he was in the transportation business. "I take people from where they are to where they want to be," he would say. That was a great reframe. The customer would ask how he did it, which would give him an excellent opportunity to discuss how image and clothing are related to success.

Small Talk

Small talk is an important business ritual. It is used to generate rapport and allows both parties to become acquainted and get comfortable with each other. We usually exchange standard greetings, talk about something innocuous like the weather or traffic, move to more personal topics like vacations, sports, or hobbies that we share, and only then get down to business.

Small talk often becomes awkward when men and women try to sell to one another. In the last few years, much research has been done on the different ways men and women communicate. A number of authors, most notably Deborah Tannen in the best-selling book *You Just Don't Understand*, have shown that women tend to communicate to gain intimacy and rapport, while men tend to communicate to gain status and power. In an average conversation, women tend to be much less direct and take longer to develop rapport. Men spend less time on small talk at the beginning, preferring to get down to business. However, they often go back to small talk later on in the conversation.

With this indirect, empathetic style, women are better able to generate trust with clients, building an intense relationship up front. Men try to get down to business first, and attempt to cement social bonds later.

When you are selling to a client of the opposite sex, keep

these tendencies in mind. If you find the small talk more awkward than usual, one of you probably wants to get down to business more quickly than the other. Try to adjust yourself to your client, so that you don't waste energy trying to force the issue. Allow rapport to work *for* you rather than against you.

Selling with Metaphors

In NeuroLinguistic Programming, a metaphor is any figure of speech or story that gets your listeners to identify themselves with your ideas. They literally see, hear, or feel themselves in what you are describing. This identification not only helps them understand your ideas much faster; it also generates emotion and really gets them to pay attention to your product.

I've already discussed how in my first few years in the speaking business, people would dismiss me, giving me the standard refrain, "You're a pretty good speaker, but we've heard all those motivational speakers before." After a while, I learned to counter that specific argument by using a metaphor. I would say, "The difference between me and other motivational speakers is like the difference between a Cadillac and a Pinto: One helps you enjoy the ride while getting you there; the other just gets you there."

Through the metaphor of the Cadillac and the Pinto, I was getting my listeners to think of themselves riding in the two cars and comparing the two. I was telling them that my message was more valuable and entertaining than those of other speakers. But I was doing all this with one short phrase.

If you can tailor your metaphor to your client's background, it will be that much more effective. A life insurance agent from Detroit whose techniques we have studied has an uncanny way of doing this. She sells a product called Whole Life Insurance, and typically listens very closely to her client's frame of reference. Then she is able to pick out specific metaphors to further illustrate her points.

Once she was asked by her client, a carpet manufacturer, what the difference was between whole life and term insurance. She quickly said, "To tell you the truth, the difference between whole life and term is like the difference between indoor and outdoor carpeting. Both look nice, but one lasts a whole lot longer and gives you more benefits in the end."

In using metaphors, watch out for clichés. If a metaphor is repeated too often, it tends to be ineffective in evoking emotion and understanding. You want your customers to think about the metaphor long enough to identify with it. Trite sayings such as "Well, my hands are tied"; "This will be curtains for the product"; "I'm not just giving you a song and dance"—all are worn out. You would do better to stick to dry facts than to use overburdened metaphors.

Metaphors and stories help you sell more effectively in four basic ways:

1. You really get the attention of your listeners. They think of you as more charismatic and enjoy listening to you. It's like the difference between reading a college textbook and reading the latest bestseller by Stephen King or Tom Clancy. One may have more information, but the other engages the reader's senses. It's the same with your listeners. They won't feel as if they're only hearing dry facts.

The best-performing salespeople in the country frequently use metaphors. They know at some unconscious level that facts and logic often cause attentions to stray somehow, and that metaphors make people fascinated with even boring subjects.

2. Metaphors simplify ideas. Even the very brightest people love simple, easy-to-understand concepts.

3. Metaphors touch the emotions of your listeners. If you use the right metaphor to get your clients to put themselves in the picture, they are much more likely to understand the value a product has for them.

4. Metaphors are memorable. Probably the best reason they

work is that your customers may forget the facts, but they will remember the stories and illustrations that you used in describing your product to them.

If you don't consider yourself a good storyteller, you may think the use of metaphors is not for you. But try this: During the next two days, whenever you explain something that is even remotely difficult to understand, try to create a metaphor from your listener's point of view. You'll discover that you have a vast store of images, sounds, and feelings that you can connect to what you are talking about. Some of your metaphors may at first sound rather flat or awkward, but when they work, they're very effective.

Metaphors become much more powerful when you can actually put your clients in a specific situation that allows them to identify with your product. In 1992, *Success* magazine interviewed some supersellers in various industries, asking them about the secrets of their success. One of them was car salesman Bill Smith. At that time, he had been the top salesman at Buick's Chicago division for five years running.

One of the techniques that Smith uses to increase sales is to lead the test drive through a specific route. "We drive through a neighborhood where there is nothing but new cars," he told the magazine. "I want my customers to see other new cars. Then they won't feel left out." By doing this, he is letting his customers identify with the owners of other new cars, which gets them to want to buy as well. In this case, Smith creates the metaphor by actually putting the customers in the specific situation. In 1991, it helped him sell more cars than anyone else in his division.

Lee Iacocca, the previous head of Chrysler, has been a master at using metaphor throughout his career. In 1956, when he was at Ford, he came up with the "56 for 56" campaign, which allowed people to buy a 1956 Ford for fifty-six dollars a month. This slogan linked buying a new car with affordability, and sent Iacocca's division from thirty-second place in the nation to first place. In 1961, he recognized the importance of linking the Ford name with the dazzle of sports and came up with the "Punt, Pass, and Kick" program, which gave kids the opportunity to participate in various sporting events at Ford dealerships. One of his greatest successes was the introduction of Ford's Mustang in 1964. At that point, the sporty European car was capturing the public's imagination. To give his new car cachet and a more cosmopolitan feel, Iacocca had it introduced at the New York World's Fair.

But Iacocca's most successful selling job was convincing Congress to give the ailing Chrysler Corporation government aid. Iacocca had become chairman of Chrysler in 1978. Because of the economic slump and the rising tide of imported cars, American car makers were in trouble. Chrysler was particularly hard hit. In 1979, Iacocca began his campaign to get one and a half billion dollars in federal loan guarantees. This loan represented the largest amount of government aid for a single company in American history.

To many people, such government aid was sacrilege and went against everything capitalism stood for. To counter this perception, Iacocca linked Chrysler to the larger problems facing the American economy when he testified before Congress. He created a metaphor that made the fate of the Chrysler corporation a symbol for the fate of the entire American economy. "But what happened to us as I explained again and again, represented only the tip of the iceberg when it came to the problems facing American industry," he wrote in his autobiography. "I predicted flatly that GM and Ford would soon join us in the loss column." He also stated, "Our problems were due to a combination of bad management, excessive regulation, the energy crisis, and the recession." In other words, what's wrong with Chrysler is what's wrong with the U.S. economy.

By linking Chrysler to the National interest, Iacocca got the senators and congressmen to identify with its problems. The strategy worked, and in December of that year, Iacocca got the loan guarantees he was looking for.

When you can learn to read others' nonverbal signals and communicate back to them in the same way, you take rapport to a very deep level.

CHAPTER FIVE

Mirroring: Building Trust Nonverbally

In a landmark project conducted at the University of Utah in the late seventies, videotape studies were done of parents bringing their children to school. One sequence involved a father and daughter. The father brought his daughter to the door and opened it for her. Before going inside, the little girl turned around to wave good-bye to him. He waved back, and then she turned around again and went inside. The father closed the door and left. The entire sequence took about three seconds and there seemed to be nothing extraordinary about it.

When viewed in slow motion, however, the film revealed some very interesting interactions. When the daughter turned to wave good-bye to her father, she began to approach him. At the very same moment, the father raised his hand. The author of the study writes that this movement was not only the beginning of the father's own wave, but that it resembled the motion of a policeman stopping traffic at an intersection. The effect on the little girl seemed to be the same. She stopped moving forward just as the palm of her father's hand was facing her. At the end of his wave, when the father began putting his hand down, she turned around to head back inside the school.

To the author, viewing the film in slow motion made it seem as though the father was literally pushing his daughter away. "Even though there is no actual physical connection between father and daughter," he wrote, "they look like puppets that are being manipulated by the same strings." Furthermore, in reviewing the entire sequence, he realized that this particular father was in a hurry, so it was more important for him to get his daughter inside the school and be on his way.

This brief sequence shows how we communicate without words. At an unconscious level, we actually mirror and match each other's movements as we send and receive information. When you can learn to read others' nonverbal signals and communicate back to them in the same way, you take rapport to a very deep level. And as you will see later on in the book, you can actually use such physical techniques to pace your meeting and lead your customer to the point of buying.

Studies of nonverbal signals have shown how powerful unconscious communication really is. If I had to choose one thing that helps the supersellers do so well, this would be it. Without even realizing it, they mirror their clients and match their movements at every opportunity. It's what gives them such high rapport with their clients and lays the groundwork for their seemingly effortless sales later on.

Mirroring

Mirroring, or matching body movements, is both a byproduct of having very high rapport with a client, and a technique that increases it. When two people enjoy each other's company, they come closer together, lean forward, their faces and bodies practically touching. If one person crosses his legs, the other does, too. If one puts her hands on the table, the other does the same.

In videotape studies that we have conducted, we have noticed that when people are getting along, they not only match body movement but voice tone and speed as well. It's as if they are trying to be more like each other, hoping to cut out all differences. To really see mirroring in action, watch two people who are in love. They gaze into each other's eyes, stay as close together as possible, and mirror each other's movements, no matter how small or insignificant. They create what has been called the romantic dance.

Adversaries, on the other hand, will deliberately, though usually unconsciously, mismatch. If one person is leaning forward, the other will lean back. If both people are standing and one has her hands on her hips, the other will put hers at her side. Adversaries will also break eye contact rather than allow rapport to build.

Mirroring also occurs in groups. When someone who is liked or highly regarded by another person crosses his arms, the second person tends to do the same thing. After a while, if you watch closely, you can learn to tell who the bosses are in any given group setting. Of course, crossing one's arms may simply be an indication that a person is cold, though I've seen the same thing happen when temperature couldn't possibly be a factor.

Learn to pay attention to the different movements people make when they are talking with you. After waiting for a few seconds, mirror what you're seeing. You can quickly learn how to do this without skipping a beat in your conversation.

Mirroring sounds so simple that people often have a hard time believing it works. To experience its effectiveness for yourself, try the following experiment. The next time you are at a restaurant with someone, begin to mirror that person physically. If he has his head in his hands, put your head in your hands. If she crosses her legs with the right leg over the left, you do the same. If he has his head cocked to one side, mirror that. This is usually very funny to watch. Chances are, after a few minutes that person will be doing what you're doing.

I recently heard a story about a consulting psychologist who was enormously skilled in these techniques. She was called upon by a realtor who wanted help in negotiating a fee that the realtor felt was due her from a past employer. Apparently, the realtor had sold a few properties with the understanding that she would get a ten-thousand-dollar commission. Her old boss had never paid it, claiming that they had negotiated a different arrangement.

The realtor asked the psychologist to attend the meeting she was going to have with her old boss. At first her boss balked at having a third party present, but finally agreed to having her remain as long as she "didn't say a word" to the realtor.

During the entire meeting, the consultant mirrored the realtor's boss. Whenever he said something positive or conciliatory to the realtor, the consultant would match his posture. Whenever he said something negative or counterproductive, the consultant *mis*matched his posture. After about forty minutes, the realtor's old employer conceded and agreed to pay the realtor the ten thousand dollars.

The funny thing was that at the end of the meeting, the employer apologized to the consultant, saying, "It's too bad you had to sit silently through all this." Obviously, he had no idea of the enormous influence she had over him by simply matching and mismatching his movements.

I experience this kind of situation often. I once spoke at a sales conference in northern California. The morning before my presentation, I had breakfast with another speaker on the program. Thinking about my speech and yet not wanting to appear rude, I spoke little, listened reflectively, and tried to maintain rapport by mirroring him instead. I crossed my arms when he crossed his, crossed my legs when he did so, and leaned forward the same way he did. At the end of breakfast, he said he had loved my ideas and asked me to speak to his company about communication skills.

I had done virtually no talking. Again, I saw how people "buy" from what they hear themselves say, not from what the salesperson says. Rapport—and the nonverbal communication that develops from it—is the all-important factor. Because the rapport between us was so high, I had created a sales opportunity without even intending to.

Mirroring generates a tremendous amount of rapport. Along with rapport comes trust. And when you gain trust, you get business.

Calibrating

Because it is a result of high rapport, mirroring is also an excellent way for you to check whether you are "connecting" with your client. If both of you are in the same ballpark, you can tell by the way your client matches your movements. If you say or do something that your client doesn't like, however, mismatching will start to occur and the mirroring will stop. This is extremely useful in determining what people like and don't like about your presentation.

Noticing what your customer does when he or she is interested in what you have to say is called calibration. We all notice things like a smile when someone is happy, and a frown when someone is sad. Start paying attention to other nonverbal cues as well. It usually takes me about two minutes before I start picking out different behavioral nuances. If my client leans back in her chair while I am talking to her, she could be showing negativity or defensiveness. Or perhaps she's leaning back because she needs some time to absorb my ideas. In either case, it tells me to back off for a bit.

I continue probing and presenting while trying to verify what I've noticed with other techniques. I keep in mind my client's preferred mode of thinking. I ask a question and watch the direction of her eye movements to check the truth of her statements. I watch for when she'll mirror me again.

Using both verbal and nonverbal techniques together is the heart of unconscious competence. You verify what you learn from one technique and build upon it with another. Eventually, you sense exactly what is being communicated to you.

Paying attention to nonverbal cues is one of the toughest lessons for salespeople to learn. They often aren't aware of their client's level of interest because they aren't thinking of anything but what they want to say. Remember that sales is a relationship; for the process to be effective, you want to be aware of what your client is communicating throughout the entire process. When you let it become second nature, you will be much more aware of what to say and when to say it. You'll know whether you are on the right track or whether it is time to change something in your presentation.

Crossover Mirroring

I get letters from readers who are nervous about mirroring. They think it implies mockery. They're afraid that their clients will think of mirroring as copying, and that instead of producing higher rapport, mirroring will make them negative or hostile.

To counter the argument, first I always remind them of the underlying premise of my methods: If you really have the client's best interests at heart and are operating on the Win/Win paradigm, your client will sense this in everything you do. Instead of copying your clients, you will be drawing them out. As with verbal techniques, your clients will be so busy focusing on the subject of your conversation, they will not notice what you are doing.

Secondly, for those people nervous about trying mirroring right off, I suggest something softer and less obtrusive: crossover mirroring.

Crossover mirroring is taking a nonverbal gesture and mirroring it with a different part of the body. In other words, if your client crosses his arms, then you cross your legs. If your client has her head resting on her hand, then you might touch your chin. If someone has his hands in his pockets, then you fold your hands in your lap very close to your pockets. If your client is tapping a pencil on her desk, you can twirl a pen in your hands.

Crossover mirroring is particularly useful when men and women are selling to each other. If you want to match someone's movements but feel it would be inappropriate, try crossover mirroring. For example, people wearing pants feel comfortable crossing their legs in a more open fashion; a woman wearing a dress would mirror this by crossing her legs more tightly. Men feel comfortable leaning back and clasping their hands behind their head. A woman can lean back in her chair without clasping her hands behind her head; she can keep them at her sides to show an open attitude.

Matching Voice Patterns

A number of years ago at a book convention, I was discussing some ideas with another writer. He was very successful and I was hoping to pick up a few tips and business leads from him. Unfortunately, our rapport was low. The guy seemed distracted and tired (as everybody seems to become at conventions). He also had a high-pitched voice, almost a squeak, which made it hard to hear him on top of everything else.

I have a lower, fairly resonant voice. After talking to him for a few minutes and getting nowhere, I raised my voice just a little bit, trying to sound more like him. It was interesting to see how quickly he warmed up to me. We ended up having a conversation that I suspect was much more productive than it otherwise would have been.

Your voice is one of your best tools for establishing rapport. You can match someone's pace, pitch, timbre, or inflections.

Pace is the speed of your voice. Some people talk more quickly than others, but on average, we speak at about 125 words per minute. This average also varies depending on the part of the country in which we live.

Pitch is how high or low your voice is. You can sound like a parakeet, or you can sound as low as a tuba player playing a John Philip Sousa march.

Timbre is the resonance of your voice. James Earl Jones, for example, has a very resonant voice. It is full and rich, projecting into every corner of the theater, and is part of what makes Jones such a great actor.

Word inflections also vary from person to person, as syllables are emphasized, shortened, or drawn out. Think of all the different accents we have in this country, from the clipped staccato style of the New Englander to the Texas twang to the drawl of the Deep South.

Listen intently to your clients for the first three or four minutes of your conversation. Make a note of everything you hear: word inflections, the length of their sentences, how loud or soft their voices are. Even listen to how they mark out key words. Pick out what you find distinctive, and try to match it. It will make your clients feel much more at ease with you.

This is particularly important if you sell in different parts of the country. Be aware of accents and other little regional idiosyncrasies. People expect you to talk the way they do. When you don't, your listeners are distracted by trying to adjust to the sound of your voice. This can create tension, waste time, and cause misunderstandings.

About one year into my speaking career, I spoke in a rural area where everyone talked fairly slowly. I spoke in my usual fast-paced urban style. I was thirty minutes into my hour-long program when a man in the back row raised his hand. I didn't want to stop my speech for questions because I had a limited amount of time, so I ignored him. Unfortunately, he kept his hand raised for about seven to ten minutes straight, and started distracting the people around him. I finally called on the man and asked if he had a question. He sat back in his chair, put his thumbs in his belt, and said in a very loud drawl, "Son, I like to know what you said after you said *Hello*."

Obviously, I was speaking too fast and had developed very poor rapport. If I thought I was getting any message across to this man, and most probably to many others in the room, I was sadly mistaken. I was wasting my time and theirs.

Picking up on voice patterns is especially important for people who make their living in telemarketing. Because the person at the other end of the line has nothing else to go on, your voice is the primary method of communicating rapport. A sales manager once told me a story of how he dealt with a telemarketing saleswoman who was having problems with her productivity. One day, he called her on the phone from his office and noticed how squeaky and halting her voice sounded. She seemed insecure and nervous, which was not at all the image she projected in person. He walked over to her and said, "Make the listener know you are sharp, educated, and confident. Let him hear through your voice how successful you look." Within days, her sales increased substantially.

When you are talking to someone on the phone, pay particular attention to the way he or she says things. The speed of the voice is usually the first thing you notice. Adjust your own pace to match theirs. Also listen to other speech patterns. You obviously won't be able to duplicate someone's voice exactly, but the more you match, the less jarring you will sound to the person at the other end of the line.

In the introduction to this book, I mentioned my unsuccessful stockbrokering in the late seventies. In our office, there was a broker named Sam, who did more business than the rest of the office combined. Sam had enormous girth. He smoked cigars. He had a wonderful personality—if he liked you, he'd blow smoke in your face as he talked to you. If he didn't like you, he'd spit the cigar butt at you. But Sam was great on the telephone. If his client had a high-pitched voice, he'd increase the pitch of his voice. If a client spoke slowly, Sam would slow down. If a customer was loud, we'd hear Sam's voice booming into the phone. He even knew how to giggle like a teenager. I don't think Sam did it consciously. He knew how to mimic his clients without offending them. And he made millions.

Through outcomes, people will not only tell you what they hope to buy, but how you should sell it to them.

CHAPTER SIX

Eliciting Outcomes: Discovering Your Client's Buying Strategy

When your clients are thinking about buying something, they are trying to imagine themselves with your product in the future. They are fantasizing about the possible outcomes of using it.

These fantasies are influenced by past experiences customers have had with similar products. They are also influenced by the present—what your customers want and think their needs are.

In this chapter, by learning to ask a few simple questions, you will learn how to elicit the outcomes of prospective purchasers. Through outcomes, people will not only tell you what they hope to buy, but how you should sell it to them. They also tell you how they bought in the past, and how they expect to buy in the future. In short, they will reveal their buying strategies.

What your client wants isn't necessarily what he or she may tell you up front. How many times have you walked into a store and told a salesperson that you didn't need any help, when in fact, you did? You just needed some time to think things through or maybe do some comparison shopping. As a salesperson, you need to be sensitive to how much a customer wants to reveal to you at any given time. Yet, this doesn't mean you can't use the time productively. As I've learned, even if customers tell you they don't know what they want, eventually, they will tell you what they *think* they want. All you have to do is ask them the right questions.

Five Steps to Eliciting Outcomes

I think of eliciting outcomes as having five elements:

1. Letting your client know what your own interest in the situation is
2. Determining your client's wants and needs
3. Translating needs into benefits
4. Finding out past buying patterns with the Instant Replay technique
5. Using the As If technique to uncover your customer's future expectations

To elicit a client's outcomes, you must first have established rapport. If there's no rapport, don't even begin to think about these techniques. Your clients won't feel comfortable revealing anything. Instead, they will feel put upon and irritated. Make sure that the conversation is flowing freely, and that you're mirroring and matching. Keep in mind that you are probing, but doing it indirectly. Instead of asking customers a series of questions, you are getting them to fantasize. By prodding their imaginations, you let them experience the product you are selling, rather than just hearing it described. And when their imaginations take over, they are much more motivated to buy.

1. Revealing Your Own Interest

When you're revealing your own interest, what you're essentially saying to your customer is the following: "I'm here to find a product that fits your needs. If we can find that for you, then I can earn a commission and get what *I* really need."

I'm a great believer in divulging personal information to clients. You'll be amazed at how far a little of it goes. A friend of mine recently called me up and asked if I would help him buy a suit. When we got to the store and my friend began trying on different suits, I went over to look at some raincoats. Although I wasn't intending to buy one that day, I knew I'd be needing one soon, and decided to check out the prices. Seeing me trying on some coats, a salesman came up and said, "I have something that was made just for you. Would you like see it?"

Smiling at his clichéd made-just-for-you tactic, I was about to shake my head when he said, "I have a new shipment coming next week and need to make room for it. I guarantee you won't get such a coat at this price anywhere else."

Although I wasn't sure that I couldn't get a similar coat anywhere else, I appreciated his telling me about the new shipment. He was being honest, revealing how he would benefit from the sale. He earned my trust, and I tried on the coat in a different frame of mind. It did look great, and he had himself a sale.

Revealing your interests in any sales situation is a great way to counter the feelings of suspicion clients have at being oversold, fearing that a deal is "too good to be true." In my business of sales training, I'll sometimes do programs for which I travel across the country for a comparatively low fee. I make sure I explain to my client that the reason I'm willing to go so far for such a low price is the exposure I'll get. I want as many executives, meeting planners, and other salespeople to hear my presentation as possible. It's a great showcase, and always results in referrals.

I've learned that if I don't explain myself, my clients jump to the conclusion that my low fees are an indication that I'm not in great demand. But once my clients know my motives, they are much more prepared to help me accomplish them.

A note about the battle of the sexes in regard to this: Women are more effective at revealing outcomes than men. I am talking about tendencies I've seen in my own experience and which are supported by studies such as Deborah Tannen's. Because women communicate more for rapport than status, it leaves them freer to share their own thoughts about a situation. Men tend to play doctor. If you told a man you were having problems with your car, he would probably ask you, "What's wrong with it?" A woman, on the other hand, would be more apt to say, "I had the same problem with my car five months ago," or simply, "I've had a lot of car trouble, too." There's a time and a place for both responses. When it comes to identifying outcomes, men would do well to try what I think of as the feminine approach more often. You'll get your chance to fix it later. When trying to find out what makes your client tick, developing empathy takes top priority.

2. Find Out Your Client's Wants and Needs

There's an old sales adage that says, "Give them what they want first, then sell them what they need later." Unfortunately, most salespeople don't distinguish between wants and needs. By wants, we are referring to your customers' immediate goal, why they walk into the store or sit down to talk with you about your product or service. They may know exactly what they want to buy, or they may have only a vague idea.

But what your clients want may not be what they ultimately need. Customers want you to prove, through the questions you ask and the information you provide, that you really understand the situation they are in. They hope that you, through your professional expertise, will help them sort out everything and furnish the best product for their needs.

To give you an example of the difference between wants and needs, I'll relate what happened when I went shopping for a pair of skis. I have trouble with high-performance models. Comfort is important to me, though with high-performance skis, support is crucial. On one particular occasion, the salesperson asked how good a skier I was:

Kerry:	I'm an expert skier.
Salesperson:	Oh, then you need Brand X or Y.
Kerry:	Well, I don't know . . . I find Brand X and Y uncomfortable—they kill my toes. I don't like them.
Salesperson:	Yes, but they offer the best support.
Kerry:	I just don't like them. You have nothing else?
Salesperson:	We do, but nothing that's going to give you as good support.

I was shopping for comfort. That's what I *wanted*. The salesman, on the other hand, knew his product. He realized that what I *needed* was support, and that's why he kept pushing it. But his insistence caused me to walk out of the store. Instead, he should have acknowledged my wanting comfort:

Salesperson:	Oh, then you need Brand X or Y.
Kerry:	Well, I don't know . . . I find Brand X and Y uncomfortable—they kill my toes. I don't like them.
Salesperson:	So comfort is premium?
Kerry:	Absolutely.
Salesperson:	Are you having problems with the boots you own now?

After a discussion of what would provide the most comfort for me, he then could have discussed the need for support. Having felt understood, I would have stayed to listen.

If you don't acknowledge what your client wants, you won't make a sale, no matter how much information you provide. I once walked into a stereo store at Christmastime to shop for a car stereo, wanting a basic system with good sound quality. A young salesman in his mid-twenties came up to me and said, "Can I help you?" For starters, he made things difficult right off the bat with that question. "Can I help you?" is one of those standard questions that elicit automatic responses. I caught myself saying, "No. I'm just looking," though I really did want some help.

After about fifteen minutes of looking around, I went up to him and admitted I did need help. He revealed his inexperience by showing me about twenty different models—everything from the old eight-track systems to cassette players with quadraphonic and dualphonic sound, automatic rewind, no rewind, even models that seemed guaranteed to blow your eardrums apart within thirty minutes. He showed me so many models that he confused me completely. I walked out of that store without a car stereo, even though I was prepared to buy right there. If the young salesman had been more savvy, he would have been able to make a sale instead of supplying me with useless information. He educated me for someone else.

A saleswoman in a photo shop was much better in finding out my wants and needs. I was in a camera shop, hoping to buy my wife an automatic focus, 35-mm camera. What I wanted was a camera that would make my wife happy. She has such an enthusiastic eye for pictures that she frequently puts her thumb over the lens or wildly moves the camera when she shoots. I knew she didn't want to spend time focusing.

The saleswoman walked up and saw me looking at a particular camera. "Isn't that a nice camera?" she asked. This was a better opening than the standard "Can I help you?" asked by the young car salesman. By handling the camera, I was obviously intrigued with it, and the saleswoman's question acknowledged as much.

I replied, "Yeah, kind of nice," though I felt hesitant because of the high price tag. The saleswoman then asked me, "What do you want the camera for?'' My immediate reply was, ''So my wife can take good pictures.''

After spending a minute or so discussing automatic focus cameras, the saleswoman asked, ''Tell me, what does a perfect camera mean to you?'' I told her I wanted a camera that my wife would enjoy using, something that would let her focus with a minimum of fuss. I wanted to use the camera myself, to take good action shots of my children. I also needed to take close-up shots of books and videotapes so I'd have something to show during my various speaking engagements. And I wanted it all at a reasonable price. The more I talked, the more needs came to mind.

That question, ''What does a perfect camera mean to you?'' got me to think of specifics, and the more specific I got, the more the saleswoman was able to work with me to find the right camera for me. However the question might be phrased (''What is your ideal camera?''; ''Under what circumstances would you use this camera?''), the important thing was to get her customer to imagine using that product. When you let people fantasize, they reveal their needs.

In probing your clients, it is very helpful to keep in mind someone's preferred mode of thinking. Listen to how someone describes a product; how he sees it, hears it, or feels it. Then, when you are ready to present what you think is the best product for him, you can use those same predicates. This is what gets your clients to experience your products directly. Their fantasies take over and make them much more enthusiastic and willing to buy.

3. Translating Needs into Benefits

While people have wants and needs, products have features and benefits. A car runs on a certain type of fuel, gets a certain number of miles per gallon, offers cruise control, power steering, front-wheel drive. These are features. A customer walking into an auto dealership doesn't care about the features as much as the benefits that these features will give him.

A man with seven children, for example, comes into your auto dealership. In probing him, you find out he is worried about having enough space, and yet, wants the car to be economical as well. This man will care about the benefits on the right, rather than focusing on all the features on the left:

Features	Benefits
power steering	miles per gallon
power brakes	trunk capacity
color	backseat capacity
air conditioning	cost
stereo	safety

When you've discovered your customers' needs, make sure you translate those needs into benefits your product will provide them. As a matter of fact, research by the Xerox Corporation has shown that if a salesperson can meet an average of 3.5 benefits, the meeting will end in a sale. By focusing on benefits, you will be proving to your clients that you are meeting their needs. You the salesperson are acting as the problem solver. In looking at different cars with the customer in the above example, replay each car's capacity and mileage back to the customer. Once he sees how owning a particular car will benefit him, he will want to buy.

You sometimes have to be a little creative in finding out needs and translating them into benefits. I was looking for a house once, and told the realtor the model of the house I wanted, which was called a Greenbrier, and the neighborhood I wanted to live in. Because no Greenbriers had *For Sale* signs in that particular community, the realtor canvassed the neighborhood, simply asking their owners if they wanted to sell.

This realtor did not exploit the situation to its fullest. Out of forty-three Greenbrier owners, she found only two who were even willing to talk to her. Instead of merely asking the Greenbrier owners if they wanted to sell their house, she could have approached them as follows: ''I have a client who is interested in buying your Greenbrier. Have you thought of moving to a different location or owning a different kind of house?'' Or, ''What are your plans for the next five years? Where would you like to live? Have you thought of an investment?'' Or, ''Have you considered other houses in the neighborhood? I would like to help you find your next house.''

Research statistics on relocation show that people tend to move every five to seven years. If this realtor had been able to get the owners of those Greenbriers to fantasize about their needs, and the benefits of moving, she might have made a sale more easily. Not only that; she would have picked up two commissions, one for brokering our sale and another one for finding a new place for the previous owners.

4. Instant Replay

One of the fundamental beliefs of modern psychology is that people typically change very little through the years. Our basic patterns of behavior are set very early in life. And they significantly influence us throughout our later years. Just think of habits you've tried to break. As a friend of mine who has tried quitting smoking said once, ''Quitting isn't hard. I've quit seventeen times.''

The fact is, we don't like change. Most psychologists believe that basic personality patterns are set in the first few years of life. Those patterns are significant in determining how you will react to various situations in later years. Obviously, maturity sets in and some behavioral responses do change, but they are minimal. Many studies have shown that if too much change is going on in someone's life, it causes so much stress that the person develops headaches, ulcers, even heart problems.

Buying patterns are no different. People tend to buy the way they bought in the past, unless something traumatic has happened to change their behavior patterns. If you could find out how your client bought a product in the past, all you would have to do is replay that strategy back to him in selling your own product. If your client says no, he would in effect be denying himself.

To use the Instant Replay technique, ask your client such simple questions as: "What made you buy this product before?" or "How did you decide to buy this product in the past?" or "Why did you buy such-and-such previously?"

I know a travel agent who uses this technique all the time, because she finds it so effortless. For example, a couple might come in shopping for a trip on a particular cruise line. Before telling them whether she has anything available, the agent asks them a few further questions. The conversation usually goes something like this:

Agent:	Have you ever taken a cruise on this line before?
Husband:	Yes, about ten years ago.
Agent:	Where to?
Husband:	St. Thomas and Puerto Rico.
Wife:	We had a great time. We really felt relaxed and got to see a lot.
Agent:	So the combination of relaxing and sightseeing is important?
Husband:	Absolutely. But it wasn't just that. We really felt well-treated by the crew. They went out of their way to be helpful.
Wife:	One day we hit some pretty rough weather, and I was a nervous wreck. One

> of the stewards spent what seemed like hours with us, explaining all the safety features, and why there was nothing to be afraid of, and just making us feel comfortable.

If the agent doesn't have a cruise on that particular line, which happens often enough, she uses the information she has gathered from her "interview" to sell a line with a similar reputation. In the case above, by asking the couple how they had bought previously, she has found out that the balance of sightseeing and relaxation is important, as well as the attitude of the crew (as opposed to the entertainment, the decor, the food, and a lot of other things that might have been stressed). If she had asked the couple point-blank what they wanted, it would probably have taken them longer to answer, and they wouldn't have been so clear about what was most important to them.

Once clients give you their answer, tailor the product you are selling to meet those concerns. If you're selling life insurance, for example, your client may say he bought his previous policy because he needed more coverage for his family. Typically, he would still have the same concerns, so you would emphasize the needs of his family in presenting your own product. If you were selling securities, your client might say she bought securities previously because of track record, or she recognized the company name, or wanted to see high growth. By eliciting these responses, you're really getting your client to give you her buying strategy. It's very effective because it's so simple.

Another useful question to ask is, "If you did it all over again, what would you change in this product?" Not only will you find out what's on your customer's mind, you'll get some ideas on how to improve what you're selling. Think of the computer industry in the last few years, and the phenomenal growth of software suppliers like Microsoft with its Windows program or word-processing packages like WordPerfect. The companies that have done best are the ones that have listened to their customers and kept adapting to meet their needs. They've learned to incorporate these same basic techniques on a much bigger scale.

When you have earned your clients' trust, they are usually very willing to answer all your questions. I was once discussing the possibility of conducting some training of brokers with the president of a financial services company. The president, whom I'll call Charles, told me that in the past he had used a psychologist who concentrated on self-image. I used the Instant Replay technique, asking Charles how he had decided to use the psychologist in the first place. Charles told me the psychologist was referred to him by one of his brokers. I asked if he thought the sessions were successful. He said he did, emphasizing the fact that the brokers enjoyed the psychologist's humorous speaking style and the use of stories to illustrate ideas. I kept probing, asking Charles what he personally liked about the presentations. He couldn't think of anything, but did remember that the psychologist was willing to prorate travel expenses to the various offices. This led him to another problem. He said he hoped that whoever was conducting the sessions this time would be able to tailor his message a bit more specifically toward financial services, rather than just selling in general.

When I put my own presentation together, I used the information that Charles had given me. I chose recommendation letters that addressed his main concerns. *I made sure that the strategy he had given me was the strategy I was giving him.* By doing so, I was able to present myself in the best possible manner as far as Charles was concerned. It's what gave me the edge in selling my services to him.

5. As If

One of the major problems in trying to determine outcomes is that sometimes your clients just don't know what they want.

A client like this can be a big challenge to the salesperson. I always prefer to find clients who already know what their needs are and are looking for a way to meet them. Such people are the easiest to sell.

The ones who don't know what they want require more patience and some skillful probing. This is why the As If technique is so useful. With this technique, you ask a question in which your customers are forced to determine the outcome. They put themselves in the future, clarifying their own needs and revealing them to you.

The As If technique is also very useful with customers who have never bought a product like yours before. You get their buying strategy by focusing on their future goals and fantasies. By having your customers think one hour, one month, or even ten years ahead to imagine what they like about your product and how it has helped them, you get answers that point you in the right direction for your sales approach.

If you are selling real estate, for example, you might say, "Let's assume you've owned the house for six months. What has occurred during that six-month period to let you know that this house was a good buy for you?"

You will get responses such as, "Well, the house we bought appreciated by twenty thousand dollars in six months." Or, "My family has enough room." Or "Nothing fell apart." All these responses reflect different desires. One person is interested in a house as an investment, another is more concerned about the comfort of the family, while the third cares primarily about the upkeep and how well it is constructed.

If you were selling an investment, you might say, "Let's assume that you've had this investment for one year. What happened that let you know it was right for you?" Your client might respond, "One year has elapsed and the limited partnership appreciated 18 percent." Or, "Nothing happened to make me lose money on this deal. That's what I like about it."

In essence, what you are saying to your client when you are

using the As If technique is the following: "Let's assume our discussion about this product has ended and it is X time in the future. What has happened in the meantime to let you know that you made a good purchase?" In response, your client will tell you: what information was important in his decision to buy; how the product met his needs; and what he feels about owning your product. Your client has just done some future planning. Now, all you have to do is find a way to make it happen.

To be even more effective, don't forget that you can match your customer's thought mode in eliciting outcomes. Ask your questions using the appropriate predicates. ("Let's assume it's six months in the future. What has happened that made you *feel* you got a good deal?" Or "In your *view*, what has happened to convince you that you made a good choice?" "Let's say it's six months from now. What *tells* you that it was right for you?") Double check your clients' responses by observing their eye movements. Watch for mirroring and cross-over mirroring or the opposite. Remember, you have choices. Use what's appropriate depending on how much rapport you've established. The more you can supplement one technique with another, the more information you have at presenting the right product for the right customer.

The As If technique is very helpful with someone who isn't clear about his needs. A sales manager for a big insurance carrier was indecisive about whether to use me for a summer training program. He seemed to have a difficult time telling me exactly what he wanted. I had asked him, "What do you really want for your salespeople? What is going to do them the most good?" He had replied, "I'd like them to become more motivated, and make more sales calls. I'd like them to work more effectively, work smarter, not harder, and generally improve their self-confidence."

Well, this was a wish list stretching from the earth to the moon. His salespeople seemed to need everything. I realized that the sales manager's response was about as useless to me as if he'd said he didn't know what they wanted.

I then tried the As If technique, saying, "Let's pretend that we've completed the program and it's six months afterward. What happened to let you know the presentation worked?" As I said this, I noticed his eyes go up and to the right. He was creating images—doing some future planning in the visual mode.

His answer to my question was that his staff's activity had gone up, and sales had increased 25 percent. He could have said anything: They were taking more orders; selling with more confidence; were better educated about their product. But he was focusing on their activity and the increase in sales.

In telling him how my teaching methods would help, I emphasized my skills at motivation and said, "Just picture a graph of the calls your staff makes. I can get that arrow up within six months."

I found out what he really wanted with the As If technique, and presented my solution in visual terms. I'm certain it made my getting the booking that much easier.

Probing with the As If and Instant Replay techniques allows you to use a counseling approach with your clients. Defenses are dropped and clients don't feel self-conscious about themselves. It's *as if* they're agreeing, "OK, I'm forgetting my role as customer or manager or executive. Now I'm telling you what's really on my mind." Your clients are literally handing you the information that they hope you'll use in selling to them.

Sometimes, no matter what you do, nothing works. I tried to sell a hundred copies of one of my books to a health-insurance executive who had previously hired me to speak at a conference. After I asked him if he wanted to buy the books, I noticed that he broke eye contact with me, saying he would think about it. I then used Instant Replay, asking him about previous books he had bought for his staff. He was evasive, telling me he wasn't sure whether such books were helpful. I thought, *OK, he didn't like the last book*. I tried the As If technique, telling him, "Let's assume it's six months into the future and you bought my book. What happened to let you know that my book was the right one for you?" More evasion—my techniques just weren't working.

Later, I asked the executive secretary about her boss's refusal to talk about buying my book. She said not to worry. A few weeks earlier, some of his staff caught him reading the book about sex that Madonna had just published. He was looking at it sideways, the way one would "read" a Playboy centerfold, obviously enjoying the pictures. Afterward, he was teased about it for weeks by his colleagues. I think that after that embarrassing incident, any book, no matter what its topic, was associated with something uncomfortable for him. My book had nothing to do with Madonna's, yet, in my client's subconscious map of reality, it was the same thing. Because he was still embarrassed about being caught with Madonna's book, he found reasons to reject my book, too.

By understanding the power of verbal and nonverbal pacing, you can lead your client to greater commitment and to the point of saying yes to the sale.

CHAPTER SEVEN

Pacing and Leading: Bringing Your Clients to the Point of Buying

When two people are in high rapport, they struggle to maintain it. Breaking rapport causes psychological discomfort, and most people will go to great lengths to avoid it.

Think of a discussion you've had recently about a controversial topic with a friend or someone else who mattered a lot to you. Your friend stated his position. If you disagreed with it, how did you respond? Chances are you used what I like to call the Yes-But approach. First you said something like, "Yes, I can see what you're saying," or, "Yes, you are right under certain circumstances." Then you gave your opinion. "But, under other circumstances . . ." or, "But, I think you're forgetting that . . ." First you agreed, then you gave your side of the story.

What you did first was pace your friend. You felt it was important to acknowledge your friend's point of view. Why? This prevents the exchange from escalating into an argument. That would break rapport and not feel very pleasant. And the more important the friend is to you, the more often you resort to this approach.

The struggle to maintain rapport is expressed in nonverbal ways as well. Think of the examples we discussed in the chapter on mirroring. People in high rapport seem to be in a constant need to match their body movements. Lovers do it to a great degree.

I remember an incident from graduate school that showed how powerful the urge to maintain rapport really can be. We were studying behavior modification. One of our professors bragged about the control she had over other people by giving and withholding rewards. But this same professor, who believed so much in her superior ability to control others, soon learned what control was really all about.

My classmates and I decided to give and withhold rapport depending on where the teacher stood in the room. During one of her lectures, we gave her rapt attention every time she moved to her right. We all looked down or the other way whenever she moved to her left. This continued for about ten minutes. We noticed that the teacher became nervous every time we broke rapport and increased her rate of speech and pitch. At times she even seemed to forget what she was saying. After twenty more minutes of being reinforced by her movements to the right, she was nearly out the door. We all started to laugh, and she asked us what was going on. One student told her, "Look where you're standing. Did you notice any connection between our eye contact during your lecture and your distance to the door?" She realized what we had done and started laughing, too.

Understanding the power of verbal and nonverbal pacing is very useful in any sales situation. You can make your meeting go as quickly or slowly as you need to, depending on how your client is reacting to what you say or do. Even more important, you can then lead your client to greater commitment and to the point of making the sale. It gives you a lot of control over the momentum of your meeting.

To visualize how pacing and leading work, think of the long-distance cross-country race. In every race, there is usually a runner who sets the pace. This does not mean that he is necessarily in front. Rather, he is the person the rest of the runners try to keep up with. They strive to stay neck-and-neck with him in an effort to prevent him from spurting ahead and winning the race.

When the pace-setting runner feels the time is right, he suddenly puts on steam and moves ahead of the pack. Now he is leading the other runners as they strive to keep up with him. If he has chosen the right time to spurt ahead, he stays in front and wins.

Nonverbal Pacing

Recently, I sat in on a meeting between a financial planner and one of his clients. In the middle of the meeting, I noticed that the client was sitting all the way back in her chair. The planner was leaning back in his chair as well. After a few minutes, the planner suddenly leaned forward and started talking about the goals he wanted to accomplish in that meeting.

Within about three minutes, the client leaned forward as well. I could tell they were hitting it off, feeling a lot of trust in each other and working toward common goals. Closing the sale at that point was almost a shoe-in.

Whether consciously or not, the planner leaned forward because he sensed it was time. He knew that if he could get his client to lean forward, too, she would be communicating enthusiasm for what the planner was proposing. He had paced himself properly, and now he was leading his client into the sale.

The interesting thing about matching body movements is that if rapport is high enough, your clients will continue to follow your lead. When you notice that this is happening, you can take your meeting into whatever direction you think is appropriate. It gives you a lot of leeway to probe more deeply, throw out ideas and suggestions, or close the sale.

You may wonder whether the client in the above example sat

forward because she was enthusiastic, or whether the enthusiasm followed when she sat forward? Let me answer with another question: Do you smile because you're happy, or does happiness follow when you smile? Many people say it works both ways. Just try smiling right now. It's hard to feel bad when you do that, isn't it? If you can lead your clients into matching your body movements, you can increase their motivation and enthusiasm.

Think back to the exercise in the restaurant in which you mirrored a friend's movements. Do the same thing, but now, after a few minutes of mirroring, change something. Try moving your head in the opposite direction. Put your feet flat on the floor if your friend's legs are crossed. Uncup your hand from under your chin if your friend is cupping hers. If you've done a good enough job of establishing rapport, your friend will follow your lead in a matter of minutes.

In the introduction, I described how John Milam, the salesman from Knoxville, got ten minutes of his client's time, even though his client was late and in no mood to talk about Milam's insurance plan. What's more, after that ten minutes, he made a sale. Milam wrote me a letter describing what happened. It was one of the best cases of mirroring and leading that I've ever heard about.

They both walked into the client's office. The client sat at his desk, and John sat in a chair in front of the desk. The client, still uninterested, crossed his arms and legs and said, "You've got ten minutes. What's up?" Milam started talking and at the same time, crossed his own arms and legs.

After four or five minutes, the client seemed to get more abrasive and crossed his legs even more tightly. He then interlocked his fingers behind his head and leaned back in his chair. Guess what Milam did? He crossed his legs more tightly, leaned back, and interlocked his fingers behind his head.

"Kerry," John wrote to me, "we looked like a couple of plucked chickens." Then, Milam did something foolish yet brilliant. He broke rapport and leaned forward—so far forward that he was leaning over his client's desk. As anyone who has read about the concept of personal space knows, a person's desk is considered sacred. You don't cross that line unless you have a good reason to do so.

Milam's timing was perfect. Within a few seconds, his client leaned forward in his own chair and over his desk. Milam then looked him straight in the eye and said, "Your birthday is next week. Let's get this done right now." The client smiled and said, "Great. Let's do it."

In order for the client to buy, Milam had to know as much about people skills as he did about the merits of his product. I'm sure that while Milam was mirroring him, he was also pacing him verbally, using all the techniques we have already discussed. His use of his client's birthday, which he knew from previous dealings with him, was timed perfectly, too. But the mirroring was what really did it. Leaning over the desk was a very powerful statement. By leaning over, too, the client showed Milam that he was highly motivated. It's what we salespeople happily refer to as a buying signal.

I recently read about an interesting pacing technique adopted by a top realtor working for a firm in New Jersey. Standard operating procedure for most realtors when showing a house is to introduce themselves to the clients, hand out specifications or any other pertinent information, and then show the clients around. This realtor does something different.

Before even saying hello, she tries to assess the mood and physical stance of her clients as they walk through the door. Adopting a stance as similar to theirs as possible, she greets them in a tone of voice that seems appropriate. Then, instead of sticking to a prearranged plan, she lets them walk through the house until she senses that they are taken with a particular feature. Maintaining voice and posture that matches theirs, she asks them a question related to that feature. "Do you have use for a spare room like this?" Or, "Isn't it nice to have so much space in the entryway?" Feeling more comfortable with her approach than with what they perceive as the more indifferent or hard-sell approaches of her competitors, potential buyers gravitate to her. She earns their trust, and gets more business.

Verbal Pacing

Verbal pacing works like nonverbal pacing, except that you are not mirroring your clients' posture or gestures. Instead, you are mirroring what you think is on their minds.

How do you know what someone is thinking about? Let your common sense guide you. You'll realize you have a pretty good idea in any given situation. If you're selling clothes in a department store, for example, and see a well-dressed shopper, you know that looking good is important to this person. In talking with such a customer, you would emphasize looks, demeanor, how something enhances his or her appearance. If you see someone less well-dressed, you'll assume that getting a good deal may be more important for this person than a particular label or cut. You would emphasize that aspect as you help that shopper choose attire.

Pacing your clients verbally also involves giving them compliments. Be specific, picking something you think your client would enjoy hearing, but don't make it so obvious as to be automatic. If someone tells you he is a filmmaker, for instance, and you say, "Gee, that sounds like an interesting profession," it comes across as rather meaningless. He's probably heard it a thousand times. If, on the other hand you took the time to ask one or two more questions about his work and complimented him on the subject matter of his films or on something else he refers to, it would be more sincere. People like compliments—as long as they don't feel patronized.

I once heard an amusing story about President Kennedy and his skills with compliments. During one White House dinner,

Kennedy and a foreign dignitary were standing in a receiving line. Along came a well-known journalist, someone with a lot of clout who used to give Kennedy a particularly hard time at his press conferences. When introduced to the journalist, the foreign dignitary made a well-intentioned but inappropriate joke about journalists not being allowed to attend important dinners at the presidential palace in his country. "Only the best journalists are allowed to attend our important functions," said Kennedy with a smile. He not only complimented the journalist but made the dignitary feel important at the same time, turning what could have been an embarrassing moment into a little public relations opportunity.

As you pace someone, don't forget to listen to key phrases and marked-out words. Repeating them back, as we discussed earlier, is an excellent way of showing your clients that you understand their concerns.

Also, think back to the Yes-But approach of resolving disagreements. Many salespeople use it, but they could make it much more effective by changing it to a Yes-And approach. In Yes-But, you establish rapport by agreeing with what the customer has said, but then you break it by saying *but:* "I know saving money is important to you, *but* don't you agree that spending a little more up front will pay off in the long run?" What you are really saying is, "Yes, I understand that it seems expensive, but other people have never said that before. You must be an uneducated buyer. What's wrong with you?"

Use Yes-And instead: "*Yes*, I agree that it seems too expensive. *And* the reason for that is so we can maintain quality. Obviously, when better materials are put into a product like this, the costs will be a little higher. Superior quality is preferable to replacing it in three years, isn't it?" Using Yes-And preserves the customer's self-esteem. When you make your customers feel smart and build them up, they'll buy a whole lot quicker than if you try to convince them they're wrong.

Slowly pacing and then leading a person into a new line of

thinking is called logical deduction, and it works on an emotional as well as factual level. The key to doing it well is finding the balance between being persistent and not getting ahead of yourself. You make statements that your clients believe in and can't argue with, and keep leading them on to the next step.

Recently, I was scheduled to be the keynote speaker at a large sales convention. Attracting nearly four thousand attendees, it was billed as the biggest sales conference in that particular industry.

Unfortunately, I was scheduled to speak last on a particular day. Every program chairman in America seems to subscribe to the big wrap-up theory—they schedule speakers whom they believe are their biggest guns for last, because they want to keep the audience interested throughout the day and wrap up with someone who will be remembered. It's flattering, but it doesn't work that way. Most speakers want to speak in the morning before everyone has had a big lunch and is too tired to concentrate.

I knew I wouldn't have an easy time trying to make the program chairman change my time slot. With the size of the conference, I was sure he had a lot of other things on his mind.

When I called him, I first paced him by saying I had been looking forward to speaking at the convention for a long time, and thanked him for the opportunity, complimenting him on his reputation for running the best convention of its kind anywhere. He laughed, feigning modesty, mentioning some headaches he was having putting together the program for this convention.

From a previous phone call, I suspected that this man was a kinesthetic. He had used predicates such as *touching base*; *if my instincts are correct*; *I really want you to zap it to them*. I then presented my case, telling him, "If you let me speak first, the audience will really feel they got their money's worth. We can't wait to zap them with this stuff at the end of the day."

"I understand what you're saying," he said "but I just don't know if I can reschedule you at this point."

Sensing his hesitation, I continued. "You know, the other

speakers will be well served by my kind of presentation. Impress upon them that we're trying to get everyone motivated so they'll be more receptive to new ideas. I think it's something they'd be able to handle.''

There was silence on the other end of the line and I could almost hear him think. "Do you mind if I ask you something?" I persisted. "Can you tell me who you used as your key speaker last year?"

He gave me the name of the person.

"And was he on last?"

"Yes."

"How did it go?"

"Fine," he told me. He explained that he hadn't heard anything negative about the speaker, and that everyone seemed to go home feeling satisfied.

"I think we can do more," I suggested. "From my experience, instead of merely avoiding criticism, we can get people to come up and say, 'Wow! This was really interesting! I had a great time!' Wouldn't you just feel great if we could do that?"

"You know, it's worth a shot," the program chairman said finally, and agreed to reschedule me.

The entire pacing process consisted of keeping up with the program chairman on both a factual and emotional level. I initially paced this man by thanking and complimenting him, trying to put him in the right frame of mind to listen to my argument. I then presented my case in his mode of thinking and was even able to replay *zap*, which seemed to be one of his favorite little words. Because he was still hesitating, I used a version of Instant Replay to further appeal to his feelings.

You may think that it's difficult to keep all these things in your head. The beauty of this system, however, is that once you are used to communicating in your client's preferred mode and using the other techniques, they will come automatically. You and your client will be concentrating on speaking about the facts, and your unconscious will be doing the deeper work of rapport and trust. The supersellers do this all the time. It's what makes sales and gets customers to become regular clients.

You can also pace and lead someone with the sound of your voice. I spent a week in Tennessee sometime ago, speaking at various conferences throughout the state. When I came back to California, my wife told me that I sounded different. I didn't realize it, but I had tried so hard to stay in rapport with my audiences, that I actually let them lead me into a Tennessee drawl. I had begun using some of their inflections and had slowed down my speech pace. All of this was unconscious. but I instinctively knew it would be the best way to establish rapport with them.

Pacing a Group

Good public speakers, especially motivational speakers, know how important it is to pace an audience. They know they need to take the "temperature" of the group before they lead them into the heart of their speech.

People usually think of motivational speakers as full of energy, coming on like gangbusters. That isn't always true. I recently had the opportunity to watch a motivational speaker at work. As he was introduced, there was a round of applause for him, but then the audience settled back in their seats looking fairly unenthused. Many people had their arms crossed. The speaker began his speech quietly. He mirrored the audience by crossing his own arms and even putting his hands in his pockets.

As the speech progressed, he began to use his hands a little bit more to illustrate his ideas. He modulated his voice and gradually grew more excited and enthusiastic. Not surprisingly, the audience followed his lead.

When people have low levels of motivation and enthusiasm, they are irritated when someone comes on too strongly. I was once waiting my turn to speak at a sales convention in Philadelphia, when the speaker before me ran up to the stage from the back of the room, did a cartwheel, and shouted, "Good morning, Philadelphia!" Now, if this had been a multilevel marketing meeting like Amway, and the president of the organization had given a rousing speech that sales were going through the roof, the gimmick may have been appropriate. This, however, was a convention of accountants. They regarded the speaker as a clown, and needless to say, he did not make a big impression on them.

In speaking to groups, be sensitive to current events that might dampen enthusiasm. Nancy Austin, a California-based management consultant and coauthor with Tom Peters of *A Passion for Excellence*, came across this problem in October of 1987. She was giving a seminar called "How to Sustain a Competitive Edge in the Turbulent 90s." Usually, such a seminar requires a fairly aggressive, self-confident approach. However, Ms. Austin happened to be giving this seminar right after the stock market had crashed. In an article about her experiences, Ms. Austin writes that she knew her audience would be jittery. So she softened her approach, using open palms instead of doing a lot of pointing, challenging her own logic, and keeping her preference to roam the stage to a minimum. She ends by saying: "No gesture of mine bragged, threatened, insisted, or steamrolled. It wasn't the day for it."

Very often, flexibility is your best pacing tool. I know of one salesman who worked for a big motor-repair shop. He had an appointment with a manager of a shipping company, hoping to land a big account to handle all of their equipment. When he arrived for his meeting, instead of one manager, he was met by about a dozen engineers, all of whom were waiting to hear what he had to sell. This salesman knew he couldn't possibly give the presentation he had prepared and have it be meaningful for the technical types seated before him.

Instead of diving into his presentation, he was honest, telling them he hadn't expected this kind of a meeting. He told them the essence of his presentation and then went around the room, asking them for their questions. He turned the meeting into a discussion and fact-finding mission, and then went back to his shop to come up with a satisfactory plan. By being flexible and quick on his feet, the salesman turned what could have been a disaster into a great sales opportunity. Grateful for the opportunity to be heard, the engineers were only very happy to endorse his services.

In pacing my audiences, I first ask myself some questions: Who am I speaking to? Why are they here? What seems to be their attitude? What am I trying to get across? This helps me clarify why I'm speaking and how I want to present myself.

I usually begin the speech itself with questions to the audience: "How many of you know who I am?" "How many of you have read or heard me before?" "How many of you don't care one way or another?" I have them raise their hands. By pacing them with self-deprecating remarks and questions that I think may be on their minds, I keep them from being negative right off the bat. By reinforcing the questions with a nonverbal gesture, I get them feeling more strongly connected to me.

I've also found that using humor tends to loosen people up and make them more receptive. To keep them interested, I try to say something funny every two or three minutes. By getting them to laugh, I'm able to break down their suspicions and increase their acceptance.

Using humor in a one-to-one situation is a little trickier. As a rule, I use it less often, because I find that in face-to-face situations, clients are usually more intent on getting down to business. I'll often throw out a funny line to see how my client will respond. Some clients laugh, others don't. It all depends on the level of rapport we have established, and their sense of humor.

I've heard about one salesman who was frustrated because his sales pitch to a buyer at a major retailer was going nowhere. They were going back and forth, and the salesman could not seem to meet the buyer's needs. Finally, he took off his suit jacket, threw it on the desk, and said, "I've given you the shirt off my back! Isn't that enough?" That little drama broke his client up, and he made a sale. I find that if my clients do laugh at my jokes, my closing ratio is almost 100 percent.

There is one other very important element in speaking to large groups of people: being aware of group clusters. If you've ever spoken in front of an audience, you may have noticed that people sitting together often mirror one another. That's because people who sit close to each other share more rapport than those who are sitting farther away.

Mirroring groups of people rather than individuals helps you establish rapport with your entire audience more quickly. For example, if you notice that a number of people have their arms crossed, do the same when you make eye contact with them. When you see another group leaning forward, lean forward as you turn to them. This is a very effective way of pacing a large group of people.

Spending time mirroring group clusters doesn't mean you ignore individuals. When you are answering questions or are engaged in some other form of give and take, mirror the speaker and don't forget how important visual, auditory, and kinesthetic predicates can be in maintaining rapport. Also, use one audience member to illustrate a point from time to time. It's a very good pacing strategy for the entire group. Zeroing in on one person keeps everyone else on their toes and makes the entire group feel involved in your presentation.

Breaking Rapport

Breaking rapport is an element of leading. For example, John Milam was able to bring his client to the point of sale by leaning over his desk. Because the rapport with his client was great enough, he was able to lead him by doing something that normally would be perceived as rather aggressive.

There are other situations when you may want to break rapport. What if your customer becomes too talkative or goes off on tangents while you are trying to sell something to her? What if she wants to discuss particular topics that you know will take up a lot of valuable time? Although you'd probably like to, in such situations you can't say, "Let's get back to the subject at hand," or "Hey, let's stay on track, Okay?" Breaking rapport does just that, but in a way without your ever appearing rude.

One of the best ways you can do this is to simply mismatch body posture when you want to redirect the conversation. If your client crosses her legs, uncross yours. If she talks quickly, you slow down. At the same time, begin talking about what you want to discuss. Your client will never realize that you have terminated that phase of the conversation.

Breaking rapport is often useful with someone who is being particularly negative, either about himself or your product. "I'm having trouble getting appointments—I can't convince people to buy," is a complaint I often hear from other salespeople. Sometimes, I think their problems are deeper and agree that they should change professions. Other times, they are just going through a bad patch, as we all do. To try and help them out of that blue funk, I use mirroring to help me in my arguments. I first pace people in as many verbal and nonverbal ways as I can. Then I start breaking rapport by mismatching and leading them to consider a more positive outlook. Sometimes, I have to do it in small steps, breaking rapport a number of times before I feel ready to lead them on to something more positive.

Rapport breaks are often used by business people to sabotage meetings. I've heard many stories of meetings between salespeople and business executives that ended badly because one or two of the executives would purposely mismatch and break rapport after it had been established.

I've heard about one such meeting that involved the sale of a pension plan to a group of company executives. One of the executives of this particular company wanted another firm to be a provider of the service. He had a sales contact there, and this vendor had not been included in the company's list of choices.

At first, while the presentation was going on, this negative executive was fairly attentive. But toward the end of the presentation, when everybody else seemed to be leaning forward in a buying posture, this executive did just the opposite. He leaned back away from the table with his arms crossed. He crossed his legs. He avoided eye contact with the salesperson. He was almost rude. When the other executives around the table sensed this person break rapport, they grew unsettled as well. The sale was lost.

A similar situation happened to me when I gave a sales seminar at a printing company a few years ago. Most of the salespeople were sitting on one side of the room; they seemed attentive, smiling, nodding, raising their hands and listening to what I was saying. On the other side of the room were the staff employees who were told to attend the meeting and weren't given a choice. I could tell that one woman, a member of the auditing department, was very antagonistic. She avoided eye contact with me, she looked bored, and after I'd make a point, she would often lean over and whisper to the person next to her. I could just imagine her saying something like, "This is ridiculous. How can you listen to this man?"

I decided to pace her so that I wouldn't lose the rest of my audience as well. At one point during my presentation, I walked over to her, got very close, and whispered: "You seem really upset. To tell you the truth, I would be, too, if I were you. I can't believe they told you to be here when you have so much work to do back at the office. If you don't mind, would you give me a candid critique after we're done? I'd really appreciate your advice on how I can improve my speech."

My first inclination would have been to say to this woman, "Do you really want to stay here? If you don't want to be here, why don't you leave?" But just as in aikido, a Japanese art of self-defense in which you use the concept of nonresistance to immobilize an opponent, I've learned that you don't hit your opponents in the face. If they rush at you, you let them keep coming and use their own momentum to redirect their attitudes toward another area.

It certainly worked with this woman. I've never seen anyone become so attentive. Evidently, she had not brought a notebook, because I saw her begin taking notes on napkins. She stopped disrupting her colleagues—and me from then on—and my presentation went smoothly. (P.S. I never did ask her for the critique, and she never approached me with one.)

In pacing this woman, I had to risk breaking rapport with the rest of the group. In this situation, I used a rather extreme measure. Sometimes, you can bring negative people back into the fold simply by mirroring them and establishing eye contact from time to time. The risk, of course, is that it can become counterproductive: You win back one person in the audience, and lose everyone else. Once you feel that you've established some sort of contact, don't linger for more than a few seconds. Break rapport and switch back to the group.

Anchoring

One of the most effective ways to bring customers to the point of sale is to use the technique of anchoring. Anchoring is defined as eliciting memories in people by using verbal or nonverbal cues. Put another way, with anchoring, you use certain words or gestures so that your customer associates them with a pleasurable emotion. Then, at a critical point, you bring back that emotion with the particular word or gesture you used in your anchor.

Anchoring is great for motivation and for making yourself very persuasive. You can generate emotional responses in your customers very quickly. Through your use of anchoring, customers will be more receptive to you, because you will remind them of what's positive about your product.

One of the most effective anchors I've seen in recent years was used by Ross Perot. We've already discussed his effectiveness during the 1992 presidential debates, when he entertained everyone with his jokes, word play, and other auditory techniques. You may remember that at one point during the debates, while talking about ways to cut the deficit, he said, "If there's a better way, I'm all ears." As he said this, he brought both hands up to his ears, which are rather prominent. The audience roared.

With that simple gesture, he reinforced the idea that he really was listening to the voters and addressing the issues they wanted addressed. Most people couldn't remember his specific proposals, but the idea that he was all ears was firmly anchored in their minds. Because television is a visual medium, the technique worked on a visual level as well. The line was picked up by the media the next day, and that image of Perot as the master listener reverberated throughout the rest of the campaign.

Johnny Carson used to anchor his audience with a golf swing. He never had to say, "Let's go." When he swung his imaginary golf club, we all knew what would happen. Don Shula, the coach of the Miami Dolphins, crosses his arms and looks down at the ground. No one has to tell the players that heads will roll Monday morning.

Anchoring can be done with words. Think back to George Bush's ill-fated "Read my lips" campaign promise. Those words brought back memories of Bush eventually raising taxes, and every candidate used the line, hoping to remind voters why they should vote for them instead of George Bush.

Joan Rivers uses the line, "Can we talk?" At one time in her career, she made an incredibly funny punch line out of those words. Now, as soon as she says them, people laugh, expecting something funny to come out of her mouth. She has anchored laughter through that one phrase.

The best time to create an anchor is when rapport is at its peak. You can use key words and marked-out phrases, smile, point a finger, raise your eyebrows, or snap your fingers. Then you can bring back that high rapport instantly by using the same verbal or nonverbal cue when the time is right.

A friend who is a financial planner told me that in the middle of a conversation with a client about tax shelters, his client informed him that security was more important to him than taking risks. My friend repeated the client's desire for an investment with low risk. As he did so, he raised his eyebrows.

Then, later during the presentation, my friend had an idea that he felt was just right for his client. He said to the man, "This fund will give you not only high growth, but it's an investment with low risk." As he said *low risk*, he raised his eyebrows. He told me he could literally see his client's eyes light up. The client smiled and bought the product.

A saleswoman at a southern California branch of Nordstrom's department store once anchored me with touch. I had come to the store looking to buy a new suit. The saleswoman came over and we talked for a few minutes about what I wanted. Walking to the area where the suits my size were located, the saleswoman lightly touched me on the arm and at the same time said that I would look very handsome in a particular cut.

As I mentioned earlier, we all like compliments. I thanked her, feeling flattered. What I didn't realize at the time was that she had just anchored me by giving me the compliment and simultaneously touching me on the arm. After I had spent about twenty minutes trying on new suits, she said, "These two really look great on you." As she said that, she touched me on the arm in the exact same place she had touched me before.

She had anchored me with positive feelings about my appearance with her first compliment and touch. She then brought back those feelings by doing it again with certain suits. She was so effective, I bought the suits on the spot. As a matter of fact, I found her sales method so elegant, I've gone back to her to buy many of the suits I now own.

Touch is a particularly powerful and subtle anchor. In an interesting experiment done at the University of Minnesota at Minneapolis, two psychology researchers left a quarter on the ledge inside a telephone booth and then hid behind a tree. As people left the booth, one of the researchers approached, telling each unsuspecting subject that he had left a quarter in that booth, which he needed to make another phone call. Of the people approached, only 23 percent admitted they had found the quarter and returned it when asked.

The researchers then did the same experiment, with one crucial difference. When they asked each person leaving the booth whether he or she had found their quarter, they lightly touched that person just below the elbow. The touch lasted no longer than three seconds. In this case, 97 percent of the people admitted that they had found a quarter, and were happy to return it to them.

An experiment testing a similar hypothesis was done at the University of Michigan at Ann Arbor in a college library. A graduate student in experimental psychology had the librarian who checked out books assume an unfriendly attitude toward the students as their books were checked out. Some students, however, were touched just below the elbow by the librarian as they were handed their books. The students were then interviewed when they left the library. A significant majority of those who had been touched found the librarian much more warm and helpful than those who weren't touched. Even more interestingly, only 5 percent of the students who were touched remembered it.

If you keep your touch light and lasting no longer than three seconds, chances are your clients won't even notice it. I've had dozens of letters from salespeople who've told me they use that technique with great success. You also have to be careful that you don't intrude upon an individual's personal space. We all have slightly different notions of where our personal space begins, beyond which a touch is interpreted as much more intimate. To be prudent, stay at the forearm, making sure the touch doesn't last longer than three seconds.

To make your anchoring even more effective, try to match your anchor to your client's predominant thinking mode. If your client is visual, use visual anchors like smiling, pointing a finger in the air, or even nodding your head. I use visual anchors in group presentations. I'll smile broadly when I tell a joke or a funny story. Later, when I'd like the group to laugh or chuckle, I'll smile broadly again. It works like a charm. I see it on their faces—when I smile, it's their cue to laugh.

Good anchors for auditories are snapping fingers, clapping hands, tapping objects, or the inflection of your voice. For example, when you're ready to anchor an auditory, make your voice go very high. Then, later on in your presentation, do the same thing. This will reestablish the emotions your client felt when you used the anchor initially.

Kinesthetics are the easiest people to anchor, because they respond so powerfully to touch. Besides your fingers, you can also lightly touch them with something you're holding, like a pencil or a rolled-up magazine. The very act of handing them something, such as a pamphlet or a brochure, can be used as an anchor. When you want to elicit the anchor later on, hand them something else. They'll reexperience the same good feelings you anchored in the first place.

Stealing Anchors

Many people have gestures that hold special meaning for them. If you can take those gestures and use them as an anchor, you have a very effective method of getting your clients to commit to you.

For example, I spoke at a financial corporation in Cincinnati a few years ago. The vice president of marketing had a very interesting way of shaking his head from side to side. It looked like he was saying no, but from paying attention to what he said while shaking his head, I realized the gesture actually meant yes.

He and I were discussing the possibility of my doing some sales training for his managers. When I wanted him to commit to my ideas, I stole his gesture and moved my head horizontally in the same manner he did. It was incredibly interesting to watch his facial expression change to one of understanding and enthusiasm. He told me my ideas were good and wanted to go forward with them.

The best way to steal anchors is to watch your prospective customers for four or five minutes and see if they have any unique gestures. Then, when rapport has been established and you have a concrete sales proposal, present it with your customer's own anchor. I've learned that when my accountant disapproves of something, he sits back in his chair and quickly moves his eyebrows up and down four or five times. They seem to shoot up like a rocket. When I try to deduct something he doesn't like, I'll copy the movement. He usually laughs—and sometimes, let's me do it.

Remember what objections really are: They provide valuable information on whether you are satisfying your client's needs.

CHAPTER EIGHT

Cashing Objections: Turning a *No* into a Sales Opportunity

A life insurance salesman told me about the following experience he had with a client. The client seemed to be matching, mirroring, and keeping high rapport with the salesman throughout the interview. But when it came time to close the sale, the client leaned back in his chair and avoided eye contact, a clear signal that he wasn't going to buy any insurance.

In speaking with the client later, the salesman found out that he was afraid to make a decision. The man was afraid of facing his own death, and wanted to avoid discussing it. Buying life insurance was admitting his own mortality.

In sales, we've all run into objections that seemed unfounded, foolish, or left us grasping for an answer. When we're met with objections like this, we often don't know how to react because they seem so irrational. In this chapter, I'll discuss how you can turn such objections into sales opportunities.

First, remember what objections really are: They let you know what your client is thinking; they also provide valuable information on whether you are satisfying your client's needs.

Often, objections are simply the result of the old problem of not listening enough. When salespeople are too talkative, they never really know what a customer's needs or desires are. They've spent so much time discussing the merits of their product, they've lost their customer in the process. When you hear an objection, always assume that you haven't listened to your customer well enough. It will put you in the right frame of mind to ferret out just what it is that he or she is objecting to.

Why Clients Object

During my years of selling, I've discovered that there are various reasons why people object to buying something that seems well-suited to them. In the first place, an objection really means that you have not yet given customers enough benefits to justify the price of your product. Also, objections can be emotional reactions. In other words, it's not the product these people are rejecting; it's what agreeing to the sale represents to them.

The major reasons I've found for objections are:

1. The financial risk/reward ratio is not great enough.

2. Your client is afraid to make a decision.

3. Your client is suspicious.

4. Your client wants absolute proof that your product is what you've presented it to be.

1. Buying something represents a risk. A purchaser wants to feel that benefits of buying the product will outweigh the money that has been spent for it. Sometimes the risks, as in investments or property values, are very real. Sometimes, they're more emotional. In probing would-be purchasers further, get them to agree frequently during your exchange that what you are presenting is what they want and need. And make sure that what you think of as a reward is how your client sees it as well. I've found that very often clients and salespeople see risks and rewards differently, and when that difference is great enough, the client won't buy.

2. *Your client is afraid to make a decision.* There is something all salespeople deal with from time to time. It's a problem we call premature buyer's remorse. All the reasons for buying a product seem right, but when it comes time to actually say yes, the purchaser can't do it. Reasons for not buying the product suddenly surface. Or, customers will actually make the purchase, then change their minds within a day or two, return the product, and ask for their money back. They don't do this deviously—to acquire and use something for nothing—but because they have remorse about having bought an item they don't really need or want. They forget about the benefits and rewards, and vividly remember only the costs.

Buyer's remorse is particularly strong with big purchases like a house or a car, though it can be a factor in any sale. I've seen this pattern many times, and have even been a victim of it myself. I remember buying a fairly expensive new computer system for my office. After I made my decision and thought I was ready to buy, I kept stalling, wasting time. Although in retrospect it turned out to be a very good decision, I didn't see it that way at the time.

To protect buyers from making bad decisions, most states have laws on the books that allow people to change their minds and renege on contracts within a few days. If you sense that a client is afraid to make a decision, find out why. It could be something perfectly legitimate. She may feel that she hasn't enough information, for example, or doesn't really have the outlay of cash needed to buy. Or, it could be something emotional, as in the example at the beginning of the chapter where the client did not want to buy life insurance because it reminded him of his mortality. If it's the latter, you'll need to present your product in a different way. One of the most effective ways of doing this is with a technique called psychological sliding, which I will discuss at the end of the chapter.

3. Your client is suspicious. Many people feel that they must put up some sort of stand, no matter what the salesperson is able to do for them. For whatever reason, they feel hostile or are afraid of being "taken." They need to prove to themselves that they are good negotiators, that they don't lose without a good fight. To them, agreeing to buy something means that they are giving in.

When you sense that you are encountering objections for this reason, you will have to use all the rapport skills in your arsenal. To me, this kind of person represents the most interesting sales challenge. Learning to overcome such objections again and again is why I determined that developing trust and keeping rapport are so vital.

4. Your client wants absolute proof that your product is what you represented it to be. "Prove it to me," is what customers are thinking as you present your product and its benefits. They want to know that it really will work for them. That's why the word *guarantee* is often featured prominently in advertising copy.

Sometimes, no matter how well you have listened, identified outcomes, and presented appropriate products, you still sense that a client is grasping for something. They're never convinced, always want more proof. Psychologists encounter this in their practice, having clients who hope the therapists will hand them rules of behavior for every situation they might encounter. In that way, they hope they'll always behave correctly and never make any mistakes. In sales, customers who insist on absolute proof are doing the same thing. They mask their fear of making a decision by hiding behind the need for proof. In some ways, they are the hardest to sell because they have convinced themselves that they are acting rationally.

Giving someone absolute proof, of course, is impossible. There is a certain degree of uncertainty in everything we buy. You can do your best to meet whatever logical objections your customers have to your product, but if they keep insisting on proof, it's an excuse. They are hiding something else. Don't get caught up in a vicious circle. When clients seem overly insistent that I prove the worth of my product or service, I try to probe further to find out what *prove* really means to them: Why do they want it? Were they burned before? Did someone rip them off?

Cashing Objections—a Three-Step Process

I think of cashing in on objections as a three-step process. When an objection comes up, pace it, uncover the intent behind it, and resolve the objection with the techniques of unconscious competence.

Step 1: Pacing an objection.

Never dismiss an objection, even to yourself. Your customer always raises it for a reason. If you don't pace and acknowledge it, you'll get into a tug-of-war over who's right—which you, the salesperson, can never win.

Your customer has a frame of reference for the objection. Use that reference point to start your answer. If someone says your product is too expensive, for example, don't argue. Purchasers' perceptions always seem accurate to them, and you can never argue them out of it. Instead, focus on the long-term value that would put the initial cost in perspective.

Also, double-check your rapport. It's important that you match and mirror during the time a prospective purchaser is raising an objection. Pay attention to where and how you're sitting. Watch your customer's gestures and eye movements. Sometimes, as I've shown on several occasions in this book, if you mirror and listen carefully enough, people will talk themselves out of their objections right there and then.

Step 2: Uncovering the intent behind the objection.

As a salesperson, you're not paid to explain; you're paid to close. As we've discussed, objections may have nothing to do with the merits of your product. To avoid getting into verbal boxing matches with clients, and to find out what lies behind their objections, first make sure that they are committed to filling their needs.

You can quickly find out if you're getting real objections or ones that hide something else by asking questions such as the following: "Is that all there is standing in your way of going along with this?" "If we get past this point, can we write this up?" "If I can answer this question to your satisfaction, can I go ahead with the order?" With such questions, you have acknowledged your customer's objection, and instead of giving him more ammunition to argue his point, you are asking him to think past it.

If your client answers no to the above questions or says he isn't sure, his objection is probably just a ruse. He is feeling something that he hasn't yet revealed to you; that is, he's not committed to buying. Go back and probe more deeply. Keep rapport high, identify his outcomes, try to uncover anything emotional that may be going on.

If you try to answer the objection before you do more probing, you may find yourself boxed in. Recently, my marketing director, Andrea, asked a reluctant client what his main objection was to using me on his program. He said that price was a big factor. Andrea then did what any resourceful salesperson would do. She asked where the meeting would be held, and offered to drop the price if it was in southern California, where we're located.

The conference was in San Diego, but they still didn't seem interested. The result: Andrea gave in to what they claimed was their biggest objection, yet, when asked to commit, they backed off. Always probe rather than trying to deal with the objection directly.

Step 3: Resolving objections with unconscious competence.

When cashing objections, remember that your goal is to select a solution that answers your customer's true needs and stays within the context of his or her question. If you show customers that you are solving their needs *their* way, many reasons for their objections will disappear.

Of the techniques we have already discussed, I have found that reframing works very well. Take a negative and make it into a positive. When company executives tell me, "We don't use speakers," I counter with, "Do you use consultants?" If you're selling cars and someone objects that it's too big and heavy, agree. "Yes, it's heavy, *and* it has road-hugging weight." If someone objects to insurance premiums being too high, emphasize that high premiums mean high-quality protection. And then let your customers decide. You will have shown them a positive side to their objection. If you've handled the objection skillfully enough, you will have led them to a new way of thinking about your product or service.

I also like to use metaphors in dealing with objections. When potential clients tell me my speaking fee is too high, one of my favorite price/cost retorts is, "Well, if you pay peanuts, you get monkeys." When clients complain about risk, I use an image of jumping out of a plane with a parachute—acknowledging the risk, but reminding them of all the protection they have, too. When the metaphor is appropriate, the client is caught up in its imagery and often takes it further to overcome his own objections right then and there.

Price Myopia

Objections based on price are the most common ones salespeople get. That's because purchasers are often so focused on the price, they lose track of long-term benefits. When price is objected to, many salespeople play a comparison game, arguing that the fee isn't so high compared with what other vendors are charging for a similar product or service. They're missing the point. An objection based on price is a person's perception that the value of the product or service is not worth the cost.

A good response to this objection is to ask, "Does the cost seem out of proportion to this product's value to you?" Then probe further to find out any needs that you may not have yet discussed.

Some people ask me what the difference between price and cost is. I explain that *price* is the immediate outlay of cash, while *cost* is a comparison of the immediate outlay against the value they hope to receive from the product over time. A sentence I use often is, "If this product performs the way I have indicated, would the value you receive be worth the price?"

Another way to deal with price objection is to link price with quality. A cardinal rule of business is that you can have great price, good quality, or super timing in terms of delivery or speed of service, but not all three together. In fact, most of the time you get only one of the three. If you can link two of them together, you may get your client to understand the bigger picture.

"Mr. Customer. I would love to lower the price, but the quality will go down as well. Is that OK?" No customer in his right mind wants to buy an inferior product. The response will be, "No, it's not OK. I need it to do a good job, too."

You have to stay firm at this point, maintaining that if your customer wants a good product, he has to be prepared to pay for it. If the customer's goal is one of low price, he has to expect lower quality as well.

If this seems a little heavy-handed, remember that salespeople often feel pressured to give in without getting something in return. You may be working from the concept of Win/Win, but your client may feel that she has the right to grind you down. Once you've linked price and quality, leave the choice to the client. If she does insist on a lower price, offer the lesser product. But at the same time, let her know that you are a professional, and the product you are now selling to her isn't the product you recommend. Remind her that you always want to suggest a product that is right for the customer. If it isn't, you wouldn't have suggested it at all.

Recently, a meeting planner asked me to do a program for

half my usual speaking fee, because one of my competitors had offered to do so. I had spent an hour listening and probing for this planner's needs, and constructed a presentation that would benefit him the most. When I heard the price objection, I said, "Sure, I will lower my price. In fact, I'll bring it down to even less than that of the other speaker. I've got a video of one of my speeches that you can play for your audience. It's not quite the same as being there, but it does achieve your goal of a low price, no matter what." The meeting planner said, "No. I think I'll take the real thing."

Disassociation

I was discussing doing my sales program in San Diego with a vice president of training for a major airline. After about forty-five minutes, it seemed obvious to me that I had what he was looking for. I said something on the order of, "Well, why don't you give me a 25-percent retainer right now, and we'll start today?" He looked taken aback and said, "We haven't covered everything yet. How can you be sure you know what my staff needs?"

Wow. Obviously, I had missed something and had chosen the wrong time to close. His mind was still on his training programs. I backed away from my statement. "I'm sorry. I must have missed something. What do you think your staff's major weaknesses are?" I asked.

You use the technique of disassociation when you've tried to make a sale too quickly. You disown what you have just said. Think of disassociation as distancing yourself from what your client doesn't like, and repositioning to what your client does like. The trick in using it well is to back off without retreating altogether.

In the situation above, I acknowledged the training executive's objection by admitting that I hadn't fully heard him out, and so disassociated myself from my premature attempt to close. But at the same time, I tried to lead my client into a discussion of his staff's needs, which was a way of maintaining that I could still be of help to him. Always be ready to disassociate if you get an objection. Nothing upsets clients more than believing that you are trying to force them to buy something. They'll shut themselves off to your ideas, and you may have a very hard time winning them back.

Sometimes, what you think of as a premature attempt to make a sale has nothing to do with you. A salesman once told me of his conversation with a buyer for a large printing company, to whom he was hoping to sell some much-needed computer technology. He thought they had struck a deal and started to finalize payment terms, to which the buyer replied, "Wait a minute. I said we needed to have more printing capability. I didn't say we were going to buy more." Somewhat taken aback, the salesman didn't say anything. Finally, the buyer looked up at him and said, "Look. I'm sorry. I've just found out we're bankrupt, and I don't know what's going to happen around here." The salesman was in shock, trying to digest what he had just found out, and it was obviously no time to attempt a sale. Instead, he spent a half hour listening to the problems that had beset the printing company.

The moral of the story? Eight months later, the buyer was with another printing shop, and called on the salesman to discuss the latest technology at his new company.

Feel, Felt, Found

This is a very simple but effective pacing technique in answering your client's objections. Here's how it works:

Your client may say to you, "It's really too much money."

Your reply is: "I understand how you feel. Other clients have felt the same way until they found out that . . ."

With this technique, you tell your clients you identify with their feelings, and then come up with a similar situation to lead them to things they may not have considered before. It's a way of building trust and countering an objection at the same time.

The feel/felt/found technique is another good way to deal with the price myopia I discussed earlier. If someone tells me something costs too much, I can say, "I understand how you feel. Some of my other clients felt the same way until they realized the difference between price and cost," and I explain the difference.

This technique is great for which one of the three thinking modes? Kinesthetic, of course. If you use it with a visual or an auditory, they won't respond as well. If you think your client is a visual, use visual predicates: "I see what you're talking about. Some of my other clients look at speakers the same way, until they find out exactly how outside speakers help." And to an auditory: "I hear what you're saying. Other clients have told me the same thing, until they found out the very real benefits of bringing in outside speakers."

Psychological Sliding

Do you ever have customers who freeze on an objection or seem so inflexible and rigid that nothing seems to work in getting them to go further? This is when psychological sliding comes into play.

Psychological sliding is a way of moving your customer from one mode of thinking to another. If she's a visual, for example, you lead her into a kinesthetic mode. As a communication device, psychological sliding appears elegant and effortless, but it's really a very sophisticated way of getting your customer to experience your product in a different way.

Psychological sliding is based on the principle that if your customer prefers to think in one particular mode, she also freezes on an objection in the same mode. If she's visual, her objection is usually a mental image of something going wrong. If you want to get your customer away from this objection without fighting her point by point, the best way to do it is to change that image into a feeling or a sound.

As pointed out previously, even though we all have preferred modes of thinking, these patterns are not fixed. They change depending upon a lot of complex factors. The bottom line is that when you as a salesperson can get customers to switch modes, there's a great likelihood that they will not have an objection in that new mode.

Below is dialogue I've constructed from something that happened to me a number of years ago. Feeling my first flush of success, I was hoping to buy a BMW and was nosing around the lot of a particular car dealer, whom I had gone to before. At this point in the conversation, a salesperson was watching me admire a model that I didn't think I could yet afford.

Salesperson:	Nice car, huh?
Kerry:	Yeah, real nice. I love the way it performs.
Salesperson:	So you've driven it already?
Kerry:	Oh, yeah. You can't beat its power and handling.
Salesperson:	Feel free to try this one.
Kerry:	No, no. As much as I like it, I don't really need so much power.
Salesperson:	Oh?
Kerry:	I think another model, something like the 528E, would suit me better. Quite frankly, this is a little too expensive for me.

Salesperson: This really is a better car. Feature by feature, I think it's worth every penny.

Kerry: Nah. I'll go compare prices on the 528E and give you a call in a couple of days, OK?

Salesperson: Well, that's fine. But just out of curiosity, if we could get beyond the money problems, do you see yourself owning this model?

Kerry: Well, sure.

Salesperson: Let me ask you something. Can you see the difference between a 528E and a 535I on the road?

Kerry: Of course. This is a great-looking car.

Salesperson: Don't you feel that if you can see the difference between this model and that, your clients will, too? If you could get one or two new clients because of your enhanced image, don't you think it would be worth the extra price of the car?

In this little exchange, the salesperson could tell that I was a kinesthetic from what I said about liking the car. I emphasized power and handling, which pertained to how the car feels. Continuing in this same vein, he told me to try it out, to really get a feel for it.

But I objected, saying I didn't need so much power. At that point the salesperson stumbled a bit, trying to convince me that this was the nicer car. My reaction? I backed off completely, getting ready to leave.

What did he do to save himself? First, he tested my objection, asking whether I would consider buying it if money weren't a problem. At the same time, he tried psychological sliding, moving into a visual mode, seeing if it pressed any buttons. It seemed to: When talking about the visuals of the car, I was very enthusiastic.

And then what did he do? He asked me how I *felt* about the fact that if I could *see* a difference in the two cars, my clients could, too. He combined feeling with image—a great way of deepening rapport with me on both levels. With that, he asked me if I thought I could get extra clients because of my enhanced image.

Notice that my original objection had been kinesthetic, that I didn't need that much power. Now the question was one of my image: He was getting me to consider that perhaps an enhanced image would get me more clients, which might be worth the extra dollars in the end.

After this exchange, we got down to really talking about money. In the end, I bought the more expensive car.

The supersellers do this kind of thing all the time. They have such a great knack for picking up on those little hot buttons—if a client is blocking on one particular thing, they are able to subtly and very convincingly slide into another perspective. With the really accomplished sellers, it's more like gliding than sliding.

There are three basic steps in using psychological sliding effectively:

Number one: It starts with matching your client's focus of attention. In our car example, the salesperson just said, "Nice car," because he saw me admiring it. Remember, don't be too abrupt and ask the standard "Can I help you?" or "What can I help you with?," both of which will prompt your client to give you a standard response. Slide. Don't jump.

Number two: When you sense that your customer is blocking with an objection, slide as smoothly as you can to another sensory focus. The same objection may not exist in another sense. If your customer says, "Looks like it's too much for me," you can counter with, "Do you feel you'd like to own it?"

Number three: Try to help customers experience the new mode as much as possible. Taking our car example further, you might get the customer to experience the visuals by emphasizing what's new about its shape or hues or interior colors. Get her to think how she would look driving it in various situations. All of these aspects would conjure up different images that would work to counter the objections.

Psychological sliding is also especially helpful with people who don't really understand the benefits of a particular product. You can tell that they've made up their minds without having fully thought through what a product can do for them. It works well with indecisive people as well, people who need to be pushed a little more. Using one of the most sophisticated but simple principles in sales psychology, it helps you counter objections without directly disagreeing with your customers.

The close is the last stage in the entire process of maintaining rapport with your client and working toward common goals.

CHAPTER NINE

Closing Successfully:
A Matter of Attitude

Closing your sales successfully is a natural outgrowth of the techniques described in the previous chapters. If you've probed effectively, found out the outcomes of your clients, and have led them to the point of buying, your close is a done deal. The only thing that can stop you is you.

Because it's the moment of truth, the close terrifies a lot of salespeople. Some of the salespeople I've watched act as though they would rather be wrestling alligators or hunting down terrorists. Whether it's the fear of rejection (they take it all personally), feeling the pressure (they have to meet some sort of quota), or not wanting to appear too aggressive (a problem for many women, though men fall into this trap, too), they develop mental blocks about the close and make life difficult for themselves. If you're one of those "closophobes," take heart. The tips in this chapter will help you relax and see the close for what it is—the last stage in the entire process of maintaining rapport with your client and working toward common goals.

To keep the pressure off yourself in closing, approach it with the right attitude. First of all, don't invest it with a lot of self-worth. If you are turned down, it's your proposal or solution to a problem that is being turned down, not you. Look at it as an opportunity to get your customers to commit to a deal or to tell you why they can't. If you get objections, use the techniques we discussed in the previous chapter to probe further.

Make sure you believe in the benefits of the product before you try to sell your customer on it. If you don't believe in it, your customer certainly won't. The close is also the final chance to iron out details. You've discussed many points while probing and eliciting outcomes. The close is your opportunity to get down to specifics.

And keep in mind that you can't convince your customers to buy. They want to be the ones to make the decision. If they feel manipulated in any way, they will not go along with you. As one veteran who has been in the business for thirty years put it, "It's participation, not manipulation."

When and Why to Close

Here are four rules of thumb that I always follow in closing clients:

1. Close when your client wants to buy, not when you want to sell.

2. The best time to close is after successfully handling an objection.

3. Expect to close each sale a minimum of three times.

4. Transfer a sense of urgency to your client into buying now.

To close successfully, emblazon the following sentence in the deepest recesses of your psyche: SELL YOUR PRODUCT WHEN YOUR CUSTOMER WANTS TO BUY, NOT WHEN YOU WANT TO SELL.

Always be prepared to take your cues from your customer. No matter how much more explaining you want to do or what stage of the process you think you are in, if your customer seems ready to buy—for whatever reason—you should be ready to close. No ifs, ands, or buts.

Watch for your customer's buying signals, both verbal and nonverbal, which I will discuss in the section that follows. And don't oversell. It's one of the most common mistakes salespeople make. Instead of taking their cues from the customer, they keep talking, hoping that the more they talk, the more they will motivate the person to buy. The opposite is true. As far as talking and closing sales is concerned, less is always more.

I have found that one of the best times to close is right after I handle an objection successfully. If a client has confirmed to me that I have resolved one of his concerns (the price was too high, the date of delivery was too far off, there was something about the servicing of the product that seemed unacceptable), he is in a positive frame of mind and very receptive toward buying. Don't hesitate to close at this point.

Another rule of thumb I follow in closing sales is never to give up until I have tried to close at least three times. Be persistent. There are many reasons why a client may be resisting that final *yes*. As we discussed in the chapter on handling objections, many people simply fear making decisions, or don't want to make a bad one for fear of looking incompetent in front of superiors. Other clients may be distracted with personal or professional problems. Still others make objections just for the sake of making them. They may need you to convince them several times that a decision to buy is the right one. Don't give up.

Persistence is especially important in telephone sales. Expect your prospective clients to be negative when they first pick up the phone. Your phone call represents an interruption to the person on the other end. As a California property manager once told me, if he talked to all the sales people who called, he'd never get anything done.

A prospective purchaser's first line of defense is to give you initial objections. I've found telephone prospects to be like the stereotypical sex-shy boyfriend or girlfriend. They may be saying *no, no, no* up front, but they wouldn't mind saying *yes, yes, yes*—if you can interest them with the right benefit.

This benefit has to be produced very quickly. It's what makes or breaks cold callers. The good ones ask qualifying questions, present the benefits of their products, and pace their client within about thirty seconds. On the telephone, everything happens much more quickly than in a face-to-face meeting. The only way to improve the high rate of rejection of about 90 percent on cold calls and 30 percent on referral calls is to have the objectives for your calls clearly mapped out. Whether it is to take an order, get a referral, or schedule an appointment, know what you want ahead of time.

In closing, remember that it's important to transfer a sense of urgency to your client. Murphy's Law states that if anything can go wrong in life, it will. Well, I follow Johnson's law, which states that if a customer can put off making a buying decision, he will. In sales, there is only a 5-percent chance that a customer will come back to buy if he chose not to when he was first approached. To counter this, try to get the idea across to your customer that if he doesn't buy now, he is missing out on an opportunity.

Look at the opportunity through your customers' eyes: What will make it worth their while to turn any doubts or indecision into a yes? It can be in the form of discounts, such as many magazine subscribers offer. It can also be creating the illusion of a loss, something that stockbrokers practice all the time. "Kerry, this pharmaceutical company has developed a new drug that looks like it may really take off. I can't guarantee anything, of course, but I wouldn't be surprised if its stock goes up fifteen points overnight. If you don't buy today, you'll lose out." In this scenario, the client isn't losing anything. The perception of possible loss is what gives a sense of urgency to the proposition.

Sometimes, clients try to get around that sense of urgency by saying, "I'll think about it." What that essentially means to me is, *no*. When my clients say they want to think about something, I try to get them to come around this way:

Kerry:	Mr. Client, would you agree that if you take time to think about this, you'll have questions?
Client:	Yes.
Kerry:	If you have questions, you'll want answers.
Client:	Uh-huh.
Kerry:	Well, why don't you tell me your questions now—I'll try to answer them as best I can.

It's aikido all over again, using the client's own logic to counter any negativity. If clients say they need time or admit that there are other reasons they're not responding to you, you've gotten more information and can use it to probe further and attempt a close later.

Buying Signals

Fifteen years ago, I went on a call with one of my salespeople when she was trying to sell a computer system to the board of directors of a hospital. In the middle of her slide show, I saw that the members of the board were leaning forward, paying close attention to her every word. This was a classic buying signal. Trying to get the saleswoman's attention, I put my finger up to my neck and moved it back and forth, motioning *cut, cut, cut*. But she was so involved in what she was talking about, she didn't see me. Not wanting to lose the sale, I surreptitiously kicked the plug of the extension cord out of the wall. The slide projector went off and I turned up the lights. I said to the board members,

"Well, what do you think?" They nodded their heads and told me that they wanted to buy the system. We didn't have to do any more selling and wrote up the three-hundred-thousand-dollar contract.

Not recognizing buying signals is one of the biggest reasons for salespeople being rejected as they close. Just like the saleswoman in the above example, they are so focused on what they are talking about, they forget whom they are talking to. Throughout your presentation, keep a watch out for the signals customers send to you that announce their readiness to buy. If you do see something, stop, and attempt a close. If you keep on with your presentation, you risk talking a customer right out of the sale.

The most obvious buying signals are verbal. If your customer makes an affirmative statement after you have presented some benefits of your product, take it as a buying signal. ("That sounds good." "Makes sense to me." "Yes, it's a good way to increase profits.") If customers start asking a lot of questions about a product, they are seriously considering buying it. Or, if they call someone into the office to get another opinion, that too is an indication that they are highly motivated to buy.

The nonverbal buying signals require a little more sophistication on your part. In general, a change in a person's posture is a buying signal. For example, if your customer has been sitting back in her chair and leans forward, that is a buying signal. However, if she has been leaning forward during your entire presentation, she is not displaying a buying signal.

A change in posture is a buying signal when it seems positive: My client looks alert and is paying attention to my every word. The client also seems comfortable, displaying an attitude of openness and acceptance. If the client is sitting in a position that seems uncomfortable, or is fidgeting, or seems somewhat unfocused, he is not ready to buy. Back off and give him room to think, ask more questions, or raise objections.

Here are a few specific nonverbal buying signals I've come to recognize:

1. The slow head nod. A very common buying signal, if your client is nodding her head slowly up and down, she's communicating that she's ready to buy. She might not be willing to say yes at that precise moment, but you've got her highly motivated. Do a trial close to test it. Say something like, "How does this sound to you?" If your client says "Great," or "Makes sense," or something else positive, then close. If she seems tentative, then keep going. If she's smiling at the same time she's nodding her head, that's an additional sign of her readiness to buy.

Be careful not to mistake fast nodding as a buying signal. The faster your clients nod, the more impatience they are communicating. They are trying to tell you that they want you to get on with things either because they're pressured for time or are familiar with your product. In a situation like that, tell them that you sense they already know what you're talking about. It's a great way to deepen rapport. Not only will most clients appreciate your sensitivity to their time constraints, they will more often than not be happy to show off their knowledge.

2. Extensive pupil dilation. When people are excited about something, their pupils dilate. Just think of the last time you gave a wonderful birthday present to your child or spouse. Their eyes widen and seem to get bigger in proportion to how happy they are about your present.

You may think that you don't get close enough to customers to notice the size of their pupils. That's not true. In most face-to-face meetings, you are just a few feet away from your customer. That's enough to notice the size of someone's pupils. If you are seated side-by-side at a table, looking at photographs or architectural plans, for example, you are even closer. When you establish eye contact and feel that rapport is high, make a point to notice someone's eyes. If those eyes seem bigger, it's a signal that you can close.

3. Gestures that show interest. When people are weighing the pros and cons of something, they often display certain gestures

189

such as scratching a part of the head or rubbing the chin. They also appear somewhat absentminded, what we call lost in thought. In terms of preferred modes of thinking, visuals seem unfocused, auditories are looking down left, while kinesthetics look down right. When you notice people displaying such behavior, stop talking. They are seriously considering whether to buy or not. Wait for your customers to regain eye contact, and then do a trial close, asking them, "What do you think?" or "How does this sound to you?"

A client can display interest by a change in his voice, too. For example, if you point out something about your service and he says, "Really?" raising his voice, you've caught his interest. He'll be receptive to a trial close at this point. If you do so and he responds with an objection, you've gained more information and an opportunity to close again.

4. *Buyer possessiveness.* In the first part of this book, we discussed how helpful it is to present show-and-tell material, such as brochures and photographs, in the manner that best suits your client's preferred mode of thought. Visuals want to look over any material. Auditories want you to explain it to them verbally, even if they have the material in their hands. Kinesthetics prefer to handle the material to help themselves think.

The way your clients react to materials shown during your presentation or right after it is an indication of how they feel about buying. Wanting to hold on to something or asking for other copies is a strong signal that the person is motivated to buy. On the other hand, showing disconnection, returning a sheet of paper after a quick glance or pushing it aside, means that you have more probing and presenting to do.

Don't let a preconceived notion of what you think your customer wants to buy blind you to any product possessiveness he or she may show. A friend of mine told me a funny story about shopping for a house with his wife. Upwardly mobile, my friend's wife wanted a house that he was not sure he could afford. They were looking at a particularly nice home that had caught his wife's fancy. She was dashing from room to room, mentally placing furniture and exclaiming about further construction they could do. She was already acting as though the house were hers.

My friend, meanwhile, was sweating bullets. Fortunately for him, the realtor had not caught on to the wife's behavior. In previous discussions, the wife had told the realtor that she wanted a particular kind of house, different from the one they were now inspecting. Perhaps that other house was even more expensive than the one they were in, and the realtor was hoping to make an even bigger commission on it. So, while my friend's wife was rushing from room to room, the realtor kept saying that there was another house he wanted to show her. By ignoring her present interest and buyer possessiveness, the realtor missed a good chance at a close. The other house, as it turned out, was too expensive, and by then my friend had gotten up his courage and told his wife they couldn't afford the first house, either.

Although you can't force a client into a close, at the same time, you have to make sure that the close is made by you. You can't wait for your clients to close themselves. This is the point at which fear often trips up many salespeople. Not wanting to seem too pushy, they don't really get the point across. They either remain too vague or hope that their clients will take the next step and say they want to buy. Always remember that while the decision is the client's, you the salesperson are the one who gets the client to that point. Think of it as the last time you will be able to lead your client—to the most important decision of all.

Closing Techniques

The following examples are some of the best closes to use. The more you know, the more options you have in different situations. Some closes work better with certain types of people.

Some are more effective when combined with others. The important thing is to be familiar with them so that you can use them when the time is right.

I tell new salespeople to practice each closing technique at least five times on a friend or colleague before they try to use it in a real situation. Paradoxically, the more familiar you are with the techniques, the less canned you will appear when you actually use them. Feeling more relaxed, you'll be more spontaneous with your client—always the goal when practicing any sales magic.

The Assumptive Close

This might be the most powerful of all closing techniques and is one of my three favorites because it is so elegant and fluid when done correctly. As the name implies, with this close you assume that your client will buy your product. Since he hasn't specifically said no, you don't give him that chance.

This close works so well because so many clients are afraid to make decisions. As long as everything about the product seems reasonably suited to their needs, they are perfectly happy not to make one. In the assumptive close, you reinforce this feeling. What you in effect are saying is, "We've already agreed that you will buy this product. I'm going to take care of all the details so that you don't have to make the effort of saying *yes*. Just don't say *no*."

I was sold this way by a fundraiser for public television. He called me up, explained the needs and goals of the station, and then asked me a few questions about my programming preferences and life-style. Then he said, "I'd like to put you down for five hundred dollars per year." And without skipping a beat, he asked me to confirm my address and thanked me for my generosity. He didn't give me a chance to say no. If he had left it up to me, I probably would have offered a hundred dollars, feeling that was a reasonable amount. But since I didn't feel strongly negative about it, I let the matter go, and he got a few hundred dollars extra out of me.

Here's another example: "This mutual fund is performing very nicely. From what you've told me, you'd do very well putting five thousand dollars in it. If you give me the name of your bank, I'll write it up for you."

In the assumptive close, I lay out the scenario and propose a course of action based on the belief that my client wants to buy, but just doesn't know how to say it. The expectation that he will buy is almost always enough to carry him along.

The Alternate or Choice Close

"Would this be credit card or cash?"

"Do you want a super VGA color monitor, or is VGA OK?"

"We can print five hundred copies or, for a few dollars more, a thousand. Which would you prefer?"

Another one of my favorite closes. With this close, you focus on one of two relatively minor choices, emphasizing a specific aspect of your product. In agreeing to one or the other, the client is also implicitly agreeing to buy the product itself.

This close is effective because people like to keep life simple. The more choices you give them, and the more consequences each choice has, the more difficult they find it to make any decision at all. This is getting more and more pronounced, as everybody feels overwhelmed by all the choices modern life seems to be requiring of them. The last thing most of us want these days is more options or more decision making.

When you close on a relatively minor point, such as the color of a product or the delivery date, your customer does not feel as though he is investing as much in his answer. It's easier to say, "Yes, I'd prefer to pay with a credit card," than to say, "Yes, I want to spend a thousand dollars for this couch." If you've done your probing and pacing adequately, your customer will be more willing to go along with your close, because you will have made saying yes easier.

When using an alternate or choice close, be careful not to confuse choices with benefits. "Should we do all the paperwork Monday at my office or Wednesday at your home?" is really two questions (when and where to meet). It takes time to sort out such preferences, and it is those extra seconds of hesitation that you want to avoid.

Notice that with the alternate or choice close there is also an implied assumption that it is not a question of whether your client will buy, but what will be bought. It's the details that you're after. By focusing on details, you don't leave room for an out-and-out *no* on the sale. If you don't get a *yes*, you go back to handle any objections that come up.

The "I Recommend" Close

This is probably my favorite close. With this close, you emphasize your role as a problem solver. If you've done a good enough job earning your customer's trust and probing for needs, all you have to say is, "I recommend such and such," and your customer will respond.

I often compare using this close to the way a physician works with patients. Even though times are changing and we are making physicians more and more accountable to us, we still, by and large, give a doctor the benefit of the doubt. Respecting the physician's position and knowledge (until shown otherwise), we follow recommended prescriptions and therapies without question. If our doctor's advice doesn't seem to work, we accept it as part of the process and await the next recommendation.

The "I recommend" close works on the same principle. To make this close effective, you have to be especially diligent in listening and probing your customer's needs. You review your customer's needs, "Based on what you've told me . . ." and are then able to say, "I recommend" such and such. If customers sense that you really understand their needs, they will follow your recommended course of action.

I like to use this close because, as I hope I've communicated in this book, I do like listening to my clients and coming up with the best product or service for them. I pride myself on being able to pick out what they really need and want, especially when they aren't sure themselves. When I feel that my client and I have reached the point of working toward common goals, I know my client will respect my suggestions. Being able to close this way is the essence of sales professionalism.

The Benefits Close

This is another very popular close. You simply list the benefits of a product, with the understanding that your customer agrees with the benefits as well. If you don't get an objection, you assume that your customer agrees to buy, and you write up the order.

A variation of this theme is comparing the pros and cons of buying a product. This is especially useful when you have spent a lot of time discussing the negatives with your customer and want to reiterate how much the advantages outweigh disadvantages. Comparing pros and cons is also useful, if you just spent time handling a lot of objections. In a sense, it's a form of psychological sliding. You want to acknowledge any negative feelings that may still be on your customer's mind, but then hope to lead your customer away from negatives by focusing on what is positive about your product.

The Ultimatum or Last-Chance Close

I find that this close works well when I have been going back and forth with a potential client who just doesn't or won't commit for whatever reason. Sometimes, it's an account I've been courting for years. Other times, it's a telephone prospect whom I've called four or five times, each time getting some sort of vague promise that he or she will think about it and talk with me again in the future. I realize it's not worth my while to keep pursuing such a person.

Although such people can't bring themselves to commit, they may be more afraid to say no to you. Give them a last chance. "OK, this is my last call. We've talked a number of times, and I guess you really feel you can't invest right now." Or, "Since you haven't bought anything from us, I would like to know whether I can take you off our files."

When informed that you will sever all ties with them, many prospective clients suddenly feel like buying. I think such people need and want the product, but are a little afraid to spend the money and say yes. Presenting them with an ultimatum gives them a little push.

Remember that in trying this close you will get a number of people who won't buy. On a straight close, 80 percent will say no. If you use this close after careful probing and pinpointing needs, only 10 to 20 percent of your prospective clients will give you a negative response. If you want to clean out files and tie up loose ends, this is a very good close to use.

The Recurrent Yes Close

If you can get momentum going and have customers answer yes to a number of questions, you can use that momentum to lead them right into a close. In the late seventies, tennis rackets made out of graphite started replacing the older wooden models. Like many professional players, I resisted the graphite rackets at first. Although graphite rackets allowed you to hit the ball with a lot more power, they also made it harder to control the shot.

I remember having the following conversation in a sporting-goods store:

Salesperson: Do you serve and volley or stay back at the baseline?

Kerry: Oh, I like to serve and volley.

Salesperson:	So you really like to put the ball away, huh?
Kerry:	Yes.
Salesperson:	And do you use a lot of topspin?
Kerry:	Yeah, I do.
Salesperson:	I think what you're looking for is a racket that will really let you put those balls away, but give you enough control for that topspin.
Kerry:	Yeah, it is.
Salesperson:	Then this is the racket for you. . . .

By getting me to agree with his statements, the salesperson led me to a graphite racket. Not wanting to disagree with my own logic, I decided to try it, and have been playing with it ever since.

This technique is similar to the choice close, in that you focus on certain aspects of your product. Getting your customers to acknowledge specific product benefits is easier than getting them to agree to the entire sale. It's like climbing a staircase: You progress from one point to the next, so the logic of the final *yes* seems a foregone conclusion.

Conclusion

No matter how well any seminar or speech of mine has gone, I sometimes pick up undercurrents of skepticism from participants as they are leaving the room or lecture hall. "Sure," these people seem to say, "these sales techniques sound cute, and even seem to make people more responsive as you've presented them in here, but do they work in real life? How much will it matter, anyway?"

I understand their skepticism. We're all constantly being hit with the latest fad or discovery, and we're all naturally a little skeptical about the latest miracle method to wealth, fame, happiness, or peace of mind. The "miracle" methods usually turn out to be rather ordinary—not exactly the life-changing secrets we were hoping to learn.

In the preceding pages, you have read about techniques that help you probe your customers, present your products, and close your sales more effectively. Why do I think of these techniques as magic? Don't they just add up to another miracle method?

You will be the ultimate judge, of course, *but when you begin applying* them to real situations, I think you will agree that the answer is no. These techniques work so well just because they are so ordinary. What mastering them does promise is a competitive edge, a bit of understanding about the way we human beings relate. And it's that small yet critical difference in understanding the sales relationship that can translate into something truly magical in your career.

In 1983, Hal Sutton, the top-rated golfer of the year, had annual winnings of $600,000. His stroke production per eighteen holes was 69.1. (Amateurs rarely score below 100; the pros regularly score in the 70s.) The bottom-ranked player won $27,000 that year, with an eighteen-hole average of 70.1. One stroke separated the two players, and it was worth nearly $600,000.

In 1989, Tom Kite, the "winningest" golfer in history, earned $1.395 million, completing eighteen holes with an average of 69.57. The number twenty-five player that year, who happened to be Hal Sutton, had an average of 70.3 strokes—a difference of about .7. He made $409,000 that year. That seven tenths of a stroke was worth nearly a million dollars.

Companies everywhere are captive to the skills of their salespeople. As the world becomes more competitive, all companies find themselves hard-pressed to survive, let alone prosper, unless they can turn opportunities—no matter how large or small—into profits. The techniques presented in *Sales Magic* provide you with such opportunities—that incremental advantage that translates into something much greater.

Give yourself a chance to let these techniques work for you. Apply them as you sell, and see the magic for yourself.

Putting It Together:
The 21-Day Plan

It's time to make the techniques of unconscious competence your own.

In Sales Magic, I've given examples from my own experiences and shared stories others have told me, so that you could see how these techniques work in real situations. If you've read through the preceding nine chapters carefully, I hope you've come to understand why and how these techniques are so useful, and why I believe so strongly that they can make you a very effective salesperson.

But reading about something and understanding how it works is still not the same thing as being able to do it yourself. This is where The 21-Day Plan comes in. Practice makes perfect, as they say. The goal of The 21-Day Plan is twofold: review and exercise. Each day you will review the main points of the techniques presented and will get to practice them through various exercises.

To make mastery of the techniques easier, I recommend exercises that involve friends and acquaintances rather than professional contacts. Completing the exercises in friendly, neutral situations will take the pressure off and will allow you to concentrate on the technique itself, rather than on making a sale or putting your professional self on the line. Once you feel comfortable with the techniques, you can transfer them to professional situations.

Even if you get stuck on a particular technique and feel you are having trouble mastering it, don't stop. Go on to the next day's review and exercise. The 21-Day Plan allows you to practice the techniques individually, so if you don't know the technique presented on day four, you can still practice the technique presented on day sixteen. You don't want to get stuck on one technique and forego learning others.

However, as I've tried to point out in this book, the beauty of this system is that while you can use these techniques individually, you can also mix and match and build one technique upon another. This allows for more sophisticated selling and the ability to gain deeper rapport. By going through the entire plan—even if you feel there are gaps in your mastery of it—you will be following the natural rhythms of your own unconscious. Let it dictate your learning curve. If you find you still can't get certain techniques after twenty-one days, repeat the cycle again. You will find that the gaps will fill in by themselves—as if by magic. But it's not magic; it's your unconscious at work. You've learned to trust it, and in so doing, are well on your way to developing your own unconscious competence.

Day One: Preferred Modes of Thinking

Review: visual

auditory

kinesthetic

The three primary modes of perceiving the world. All of us have one preferred mode, but slip into other modes as well, either voluntarily or by persuasion. Clues to the mode someone is using: the predicates used and the direction of eye movements.

Exercise: The best way to sharpen your skills at perceiving different modes of thinking is to ask people to describe something. This exercise has two parts. For part 1, pick three friends and ask them to talk about such things as the following: the town they grew up in; different family members; where they work; or their last vacation. Have them talk for about three minutes.

To pick out each friend's preferred mode, notice two things: which predicates a person accesses most often, and when he or she seems most comfortable. (Eye movements will come on Day Two.)

In part two, you are more direct. After listening to your friends, question them about what they have been describing. Ask:

1. How they picture the object or the situation
2. What sounds they remember
3. What feelings come to mind

Have them talk for about a minute, and again notice the predicates they use most often and when they seem most comfortable. You can also ask them, "Which of the three did you remember best?" You will notice that some people have an easier time with one mode versus another. Once you are adept at picking out

201

the preferred thinking modes of your friends, you will start noticing them in more professional settings.

Day Two: Eye Movements

Review: We all move our eyes in a particular direction when
we're thinking in a particular mode. The movements are as follows:

visual:	up right (creating images, i.e., thinking about the future)
	up left (thinking about the past)
	unfocused (converting words to images)
auditory:	side right (creating sounds, i.e., thinking about the future)
	side left (remembering sounds from the past)
	down left (converting words to sounds)
kinesthetic:	down right (accessing feelings)

Exercise: Ask three people to describe their dream house and
watch the movement of their eyes. Because they are creating an
answer (that is, thinking about the future), their eyes will go
either up right, side right, or down right for kinesthetics.

Then ask those same three people to describe the first house
they remember. Because they are thinking about the past, their
eyes will go to the left. The person who looks down while describing the house is a kinesthetic, and is sorting out feelings, whether
related to the future or the past.

Feel free to switch the object being described for this exercise.
The point of the exercise is to see what accessing information
looks like—how eye movement is related to the mental maps we
use as we communicate. As you learn to spot eye movement, you
can also judge whether it matches the content of what someone

is telling you. If people are talking about the future and their eyes indicate they are thinking about the past, you know something is probably not right. Most people love to practice this exercise— learning to judge the truth of what you hear gives you a very powerful tool in your arsenal of reading people.

Day Three: Listening Techniques

Review: People don't buy as much on what you say as on what they themselves are telling you. Listening effectively is reinforcing what your speaker is telling you, and hearing the emotions behind those words. Use the following listening techniques to legitimize what your speaker is saying and to create empathy.

Reflective listening—repeating words or phrases every thirty seconds or so: "Oh? So, you bought a car?" "Yes, it *is* expensive." "You got the job?"

Paraphrase listening—rephrasing your speaker's words in your own words.

Speaker:	It has room for seven passengers and gets twenty-two miles a gallon.
Your paraphrase:	Great capacity and great mileage, huh?
Speaker:	I need a lot of closets and light.
Your paraphrase:	Storage and sunlight are important.

Shared listening—turning listening into a conversation by sharing your own experiences. The more you can do that, the more comfortable your speakers feel with you.

Exercise: During the course of the day, pick whichever technique seems most comfortable to you, and use it when you are listening to someone. Remember, one of the benefits of Neuro-Linguistic Programming is to give you options. The better you are at mixing and matching, the less obvious you will be, and the more you will get your speaker to open up to you.

Day Four: Marking Out and Using Key Words

Review: To become more sophisticated in listening and reinforcing your speaker's comments, you want to note words that carry special meaning for your speaker and use them back appropriately.

Key Words—jargon, highly colorful expressions, words and phrases that are extreme or exaggerated in meaning.

Marked-Out Words—words that are ordinary in content but that are delivered with emotional emphasis. They are punched out; there is a pause before and after the word, and the pitch of the voice may change.

Exercise: Telephone conversations are a good way to practice picking up on key and marked-out words, because you are not distracted by the physical presence of the speaker.

During your phone conversations today, listen for words that might carry special meaning and then ask your speaker, "What do you mean by that?" "What does the word exactly mean to you?" "Can you specify what you mean by the term?" By doing so, you will not only deepen rapport, you will pick up information that you otherwise may have missed.

Day Five: The Fifteen Most Persuasive Words

Review: Words that bring forth positive feelings in your listener. These are words that we all hear and see every day, which advertisers use to great effect.

discover	proven
good	results
money	safe
easy	save
guaranteed	own
health	free
love	best
new	

Exercise: Over the course of the day, make a point of using at least two of the words from the above list in every conversation or exchange that you have. If you are writing letters or memos, use the words in your correspondence. Then note the response you get.

The effect of using these words is twofold: You will get the attention of your listeners more quickly, and they will better remember what you are telling them.

This exercise does not have to be applied to selling situations, per se. As a matter of fact, the more you can use this technique in day-to-day living, the more it will become part of your unconscious repertoire.

Examples of situations during which you can use persuasive words: at work, talking with your sales manager about implementing new procedures; writing memos; discussing competitors, or bringing up other concerns. Use these words with friends when making plans for entertainment, or with family members when deciding on purchases.

Day Six: Reframing and Using Metaphors

Review: Reframing is putting any concept or situation into a different perspective. With reframing, you take something that is negative or neutral and turn it into something more positive. This deepens rapport by influencing the person you are communicating with to think about a response, instead of giving you automatic answers.

Using metaphors is getting your listeners to identify themselves with your ideas. By literally allowing them to see, hear, or feel themselves in a particular story or situation, you get them to understand your ideas more quickly and vividly.

Exercise: To further increase your verbal sophistication, practice these two techniques today.

With everyone you greet over the course of the day, try not to say, "How are you?" Instead, think of a question or greeting that will preclude automatic responses. "How is your day going?" is a perfectly legitimate question. If you know something about the person, incorporate that into your greeting: "Hello. Has your wife gotten that promotion yet?" "Hi. How's that book coming?" "How's that project you're working on?" "How's that new job treating you?"

Use metaphors as well. Whenever you are describing something, try to do it so that you link it to your listener's experience. For example, focus on your listener's job or position. In talking with your secretary, describe a great sale you made by comparing it to a wonderful job he or she did for you. Or, in talking with someone who is interested in a particular sport or team, say, "Boy, I was 0 to 4 for today," or, "Boy, I'm going to the Superbowl with this one!"

As always, you aren't planning for a specific time to use these two techniques. You don't know who you will greet and when, and you don't know when the opportunities will come up to describe something in quite this way. That is the point of the exercises on day six. Instead of trying to think through your greetings and metaphors and worrying about choosing the right words or coming up with the right comparisons, try to be spontaneous. The more you can let your unconscious guide you, the more quickly and easily these techniques will sink in.

Day Seven: Review

You have gone over preferred modes of thinking and the different verbal techniques. Now, to fully review your first week of The 21-Day Plan, it's time to practice combining what you have learned so far.

Exercise: Today, you are free to use any of the verbal techniques we have already covered. But practice using the techniques in conjunction with the different mental maps those around you are using.

For example, if you've chosen paraphrase listening with a friend, first try to make yourself aware of the predicates he or she is using. Then, when you paraphrase those words, do so in the mode you think the friend prefers. If you try to reframe something or describe it in terms of a metaphor, try to use visual, auditory, or kinesthetic predicates. Even as you're listening for key or marked-out words, you can replay them with the appropriate predicates.

The choices you have are almost endless, which is the beauty of NLP. The more you become comfortable with each of the techniques, the more combinations you will be able to think of.

Day Eight: Small Talk and the Battle of the Sexes

Review: Men and women tend to approach conversations differently. Women try to gain rapport first, and conduct business second. Men are much more apt to get quickly into a discussion about whatever business is at hand, and then "shoot the breeze" in the middle or toward the end of the conversation. Being aware of the different tendencies can prevent misunderstandings and lost opportunities.

Exercise: If you're a man, try to conduct any conversations you have from a woman's point of view. Instead of getting right

down to business, try different ways of creating rapport. If someone complains that certain work is shoddy or isn't being done,
empathize, relating a similar complaint of your own. If someone
tells you about a particular problem, personal or work related,
relate a problem of your own.

If you're a woman, try to cut down on the empathy and get
down to business. Let the empathy and schmoozing come later.

If you're like most people, you will find this exercise very
difficult. I like having people do it, because it shows them just
how wide the gulf between the sexes can be and makes them a
little more aware of how the opposite sex views the world. And
the more you are aware of these differences, the better you will
be at bridging that gulf and creating rapport when it really counts.

Day Nine: Mirroring and Crossover Mirroring

Review: Observe and emulate body language.

Mirroring—the matching of body movements that is both a
byproduct of high rapport and something that increases it.

Crossover Mirroring—a more subtle and less obvious form
of mirroring. You take a nonverbal gesture and mirror it with a
different part of your body.

Exercise: Think of a problem you might have at work or at
home. Then choose two, four, or six friends. Tell half of them
the problem while you are mirroring and crossover mirroring their
movements. Tell the other half your problem without mirroring
them. See what the response is. Are those people you do not
mirror as attentive? Are they as full of advice or words of encour-
agement? In short, are they in as deep rapport with you?

Also, watch what happens to the other person's movements
as you get deeper into your conversation. Notice how quickly
mirroring takes place when rapport is high. Being aware of this
phenomenon is a great way to tell whether you are getting through

to the person you are talking with—whether he or she is really getting the meaning and intent of your message.

Day Ten: Matching Voice Patterns

Review: Just as we mirror body movements, we can match someone's voice as well. Auditories are most adept at doing this, but everyone can do it to a certain degree. The different aspects of someone's voice that you can match are:

Pace—the speed at which someone speaks. The average is about 125 words per minute.

Pitch—how high or low someone's voice is.

Timbre—the resonance of someone's voice.

Word inflections and accents—the different ways of pronouncing the same word.

Exercise: Here's another good exercise for the telephone. Spend the day paying attention to the different voice aspects of people with whom you have phone conversations. When you feel you have picked out something distinctive, try to match it. This exercise is especially helpful if you are discussing a problem or are otherwise involved in a tense conversation. The more you can match the voice, the more the tension will dissipate.

Day Eleven: Anchoring and Stealing Anchors

Review: Use verbal and nonverbal cues.

Anchoring—using certain gestures or words that are associated with a pleasurable emotion; of these, the most powerful anchor is a light touch.

Stealing anchors—using someone else's gestures as a way of reinforcing rapport.

Exercise: Try the following exercise on a few friends (one at a time). As you are talking to each, say, "You look great!" while pointing a finger at that person. Then, after about ten minutes, when there is a lull in the conversation, just point your finger and ask what that friend is thinking. Your friend will respond with a positive statement and will remember your comment about his or her looks.

To make the exercise even more effective, try to notice the mental map the person you are talking to is using. If he or she is an auditory, instead of saying, "You look great" and pointing a finger, say, "That sounds good," and tug on your earlobe. For a kinesthetic say, "That must feel wonderful," and lightly touch your stomach. Ten minutes later, repeat the motion and ask each friend what he or she is thinking about.

If you spot any interesting gestures someone is making, try to pick out what is meant. Then use it back to that person and ask, "What does this remind you of?" Most people will have no idea that you stole their anchor.

Day Twelve: Pacing

Review: Pacing is defined as acknowledging someone's mood or physical stance and communicating to the person at the same emotional level, either verbally or nonverbally.

Exercise: Now that you have practiced nonverbal techniques, you can try adding them to your repertoire. To be able to pace someone effectively, you need to make yourself aware of both the verbal and nonverbal cues the person is sending you. Spend the day doing this. Observe everyone you come into contact with, and make a point of noticing as many characteristics about them as you can: whether they're visuals, auditories, or kinesthetics; the words they use to describe things; their physical stance, mood, and the different aspects of their voices.

Practice matching and mirroring whatever you notice. Use the same predicates, key words, and jargon. If you notice any anchors, steal them. If you're discussing a problem or negotiating something with someone of the opposite sex, try to go at his or her pace, not yours.

Observe what comes easily to you, and what seems to be more difficult. When you are going through the cycle again, you will be able to practice those techniques a second time. Also notice if any people pick up on what you're doing. If they do, find out what they noticed and when, so you can be less obtrusive next time.

Day Thirteen: Leading

Review: Leading is breaking away from the pack. It works because of the struggle to maintain rapport. Once you have learned to pace someone, you can then more easily lead your meeting with that person in whatever direction you wish to go.

Leading can be done in essentially two ways: a smooth, elegant change in any pacing techniques you're using, or an abrupt change in pacing, which works as a break in rapport

Exercise: During the first part of the day, practice the first form of leading. Do essentially what you were doing on day twelve, when you practiced pacing whomever you came in contact with. But today, after a few minutes of pacing, try to slowly change whatever you are doing: If you're mirroring someone, try the opposite, or at the very least do crossover mirroring; if you're trying to match the pace or pitch of someone's voice, slowly increase or decrease it, or go higher or lower; if you're pacing with verbal cues, try using those cues to take the conversation to a new topic. In all of these cases, watch to see how long it takes your partner to follow your lead. Make a mental note of which techniques work best for you.

This afternoon, you can try to break rapport more abruptly. In the middle of any conversation, suddenly stand up, but continue talking as if nothing has happened. Notice what it does to the person you are with; he will feel some pressure to finish the conversation and may even say something to that effect. Or, you can do this at the moment you want the person to agree to something or follow a piece of advice (much as John Milam did when he leaned over the desk of the owner of the manufacturing company).

A verbal counterpart to standing up is inserting the word "Well . . ." during a lull in any conversation you are having. Do this on the telephone. For example, you might be discussing something that needs to be done with a coworker at the office, or are going over different things you might do with a friend this evening. After you feel you've gone over enough specifics, say "Well . . ." Your partner will take that as a cue to make a choice, or end the conversation. You do this naturally all the time. Now you are learning to do it consciously to move the conversation forward at the precise time you want to do so.

Day Fourteen: Review

A day to review pacing and leading with all the verbal and nonverbal techniques you have practiced over the previous two weeks.

Exercise: Pick a small project that you would like to convince a friend to take part in. It should be something that you genuinely want to do—anything from taking a vacation or weekend trip to writing a letter to the editor or starting a drive for a particular cause. Or, the project could be a household task that you and other family members have been putting off: conducting a yard sale, cleaning out closets, refinishing the attic.

Using any technique you wish, try to sell the person on your proposal. First pace those you are talking to, and then try to lead them to the logical conclusion that participating with you in your project is the best thing that they can do for themselves. The more motivated you can get them, the better.

This exercise is even more instructive if you do it with two different people. With one person, however, do not use any rapport-building techniques. Simply relay the facts. With the second person, relay the facts and use whatever rapport-building techniques you can. Notice how differently they respond.

Day Fifteen: Outcomes, Part 1, Buying Strategy

Review: An outcome is experiencing a product or situation visually, auditorially, and kinesthetically. It is a fantasy of what owning the product or being in a particular situation will be like. When you know the outcome of your clients, you know what their buying strategy is.

Exercise: Understanding what a strong influence outcomes have on buying behavior is so important, we will spend the next couple of days on it.

Pick three goals for the coming year: something you would like to own; something you would like to change or strengthen in your personality; a goal you would like to achieve career-wise. Make each of them an outcome by visualizing, hearing, and feeling the product or situation.

For example, if you want to purchase a new house, spend a few minutes thinking about how you would like it to look: its color, shape, the landscaping. Then think of sounds associated with the house: the noise of children at play; windows and doors being opened; the sound of pets in the house. To fantasize about the house kinesthetically, imagine the atmosphere of the house: sitting in front of the fireplace; sunning yourself on a porch; placing yourself in different rooms.

You can do the same thing with your goals that are less tangible, like a change in your personality. There are still many images, sounds, and feelings you can come up with when you imagine what life may be like for you with your new personality trait. And that's the point of this exercise. You'll be amazed at how many specifics you can come up with when you put your unconscious mind to work.

Day Sixteen: Outcomes, Part 2, Wants Versus Needs

Review: Choices and necessities.

Wants—the immediate goal of your clients; why they walk into a store or talk to you about a particular product. It is what they are willing to reveal up front.

Needs—something that clients or customers feel is necessary for them to have.

Exercise: You will go through the day making various purchases: milk, gas for the car, lunch, clothes, odds and ends, things for the house or apartment. During each purchase, ask yourself whether you wanted it or needed it.

Do the same thing with friends. Ask them about the last thing they purchased. Was it something they wanted or needed?

As you ask others that question, you will find that most people say they needed to make the purchase. If you get that response, ask why the product was needed, and how it will help. Find out whether there are other products that can perform similar functions.

The more you question, the more you will find that people are actually buying something they want. Need is secondary. Thus the adage, "Sell them what they want first, then what they need." As a salesperson, you always have to acknowledge what someone wants first, even if it's not what he or she ultimately needs.

Day Seventeen: Outcomes, Part 3, Translating Needs into Benefits

Review: People have wants and needs; products have features and benefits. Features and benefits don't matter to a customer unless you can link them to wants and needs.

Exercise: Pick a product you wish you had, and list all the product's features you can think of on a piece of paper. Now pick your three favorite features—these are the benefits to you of owning that product. Usually, they will be the first features you list.

Do the same exercise with a friend. Ask what kind of car that person would like to own and why. Your friend will list certain features that represent the benefits of owning that car. Now see how many other features you can come up with. Quite a lot.

In selling, you have to think of your products in the way your clients think of them. You are selling the benefits of owning the product. If your customers don't see any benefits, the product doesn't mean much to them, and they don't think it is worth buying.

Day Eighteen: Outcomes, Part 4, Instant Replay

Review: Customers' buying patterns.

Instant Replay is a technique for eliciting the buying strategy of your customers by finding out how they've bought similar products in the past. Questions to ask: "What made you buy this product before?" "How did you decide to buy this product in the past?" "Why did you buy such-and-such previously?"

Exercise: Have some friends tell you how they bought one of their favorite possessions. Ask them, "What made you decide to buy X?" In the beginning, most people will give you general answers, saying something such as, "I liked it" or, "It seemed to be a good buy."

Don't let them get away with that answer. Keep questioning them, trying to elicit three specific things they liked about the product. You will see that if you keep probing, eventually, they will get beyond the quick, automatic answers and give you the real reasons.

Note: This is a good exercise in which to practice watching eye movement, too. Since your friends will be talking about the past, watch whether their eyes go to the left (either up or to the side), or down right for kinesthetics. If their eyes move up or side right, it means they're creating images or sounds; that is, fabricating their answer. Something's not right, and you can keep probing further.

Day Nineteen: Outcomes, Part 5, As If

Review: Customers' future purchases.

As If is a technique helpful for finding out future buying strategy. It is used for a product that customers have never bought before, or if they're not sure of what they want. Questions to ask: "Let's assume it's X time in the future. What has happened to convince you that you have made a good purchase?" "Why do you think you made the right decision?"

Exercise: Ask friends if they've been considering buying something recently, something they'd like to have but haven't gotten around to purchasing. It could be anything from the obvious choices of a new car or a new house to something more personal, like a new musical instrument or a piece of jewelry.

When your friends tell you what it is, ask them: "Let's assume you've had X for a year. What has happened in that year to let you know it was the perfect choice for you?"

As with Instant Replay, try to pin down three specific benefits. Also, listen and watch for visual, auditory, or kinesthetic cues, asking some leading questions to further persuade friends to experience the desired product.

Day Twenty: Cashing Objections

Review: Objections let you know what your clients are really thinking. Instead of trying to convince them to think differently, you probe more deeply and turn their objections into sales opportunities. The different techniques in cashing objections:

Disassociation, which you use when you have pushed a sale a little too hard. You disown what you have just said. For example, you may be trying to impress a customer with the power of a particular car. You say, "This car does a hundred and ninety miles per hour." Your customer responds, "Well, I don't go that fast.'' You would answer, "I'm glad you said that. Many people drive too fast. I just used that as an example to demonstrate how powerful the engine really is.''

Feel, Felt, Found is acknowledging a client's objection by saying that you understand his point of view. If you can then remember a similar objection someone else had and how it was successfully resolved, you have diffused the objection.

Psychological sliding is a way of moving your customer from one mode of thinking to another. Useful for inflexible or rigid people who freeze on an objection in one particular mode.

Exercise: Throughout the day, watch for opportunities when friends or coworkers seem to be giving you resistance for whatever reason. It could be something that you've asked an assistant at the office to do, or plans that a friend does not want to commit to. Try to diffuse their objections by using one of the above three techniques.

Note: If you want to practice psychological sliding, notice whether someone's objection is done in visual, auditory, or kinesthetic terms. Then pick another aspect of the object or situation and present it in different terms. Keep practicing such transitions throughout the day. See if the person responds with more enthusiasm.

Day Twenty-one: Putting It All Together

Congratulations! You have reached the last day of your 21-Day Plan. Use it to practice whichever *Sales Magic* technique you want to work on. It can be something you find very difficult, or a technique you already feel good about and want to sharpen further.

Or, you can start today by committing to go through the cycle again. Remember, everyone picks up different techniques at different speeds, and the important thing is to keep trying them, letting your unconscious have the final say.

To help you review all the techniques, I have put together the following account of a meeting between a client and a financial services salesman. As you read the dialogue between Dennis the planner and Chuck the prospective client, try to pick out the different techniques. A "play-by-play" analysis afterward will explain how and why each technique was used.

Dennis:	Hi, Chuck. It was nice of Ben Lewis to refer you to me. Have you known Ben long?
Chuck:	For a couple of years. We play tennis together.
Dennis:	I used to play with Ben. But he got better and I got worse. I've switched to water sports— lying in the pool.
Chuck:	(smiling) Yes, Ben's a great player . . . .
Dennis:	Chuck, as I mentioned to you on the phone, I'm a financial planner. Tell me, what does financial planning mean to you?
Chuck:	I think of it as a way to protect yourself from unnecessary abusive taxes and help plan for the future . . . That's my view of it anyway.
Dennis:	It seems pretty accurate to me. I asked you that question because it's important for me to know what you think about financial planning. I want to have a place for us to start.
Chuck:	Well, I also see it as a way of being in better control of my money. Isn't that what financial planning is all about?
Dennis:	Yes. You're obviously familiar with personal economics already. One more question, Chuck. What do you see yourself accomplishing as a result of our meeting today?

Chuck: Well, I want to find out more about my financial weaknesses and some of the mistakes I've made. I also want to buy a house in the next year. I need to find out some ways I can use my money better in making big purchases like that.

Dennis: So you picture yourself in a new house, huh?

Chuck: Yes. I like the one I'm in, but some friends have said that buying a rental may be a smart move. What do you think?

Dennis: Well, if you don't mind tying up a lot of money for a few years and are willing to spend a lot of time managing the property, it could be pretty lucrative. But let's assume it's five years down the road. What's happened to let you know an investment like this was good for you?

Chuck: That's a tough question. I guess the property appreciated 15 to 20 percent every year. I only spent a few hours a month with property maintenance. And I was able to write off most of it on my income taxes.

Dennis: So, 15- to 20-percent appreciation, a few hours of maintenance, and income tax write-offs are important to you, correct?

Chuck: Yes, I guess.

Dennis: I had a client come in here last week, and he had much the same view of his objectives as you do. We first met five years ago—he was a teacher, like you are. Now, five years later, he's off sailing for six months in the Caribbean with his wife and son.

Chuck: Really?

Dennis: Yes. The interesting thing is that five years ago, he had about as much money as you

	have now, but received 28 percent on his invested dollars. He hasn't had to spend even one hour maintaining a rental property. Are you interested in how he did it?
Chuck:	You bet.
Dennis:	He put money into what is called a real estate limited partnership.
Chuck:	Now, wait a second. I've looked at those before. You stick in a pile of money and the IRS may just come along and say, "We don't like this one. It's too abusive." If the company I invest in goes out of business, then I'd be stuck. At least with my own rental house, I know I could write off the losses and improvements.
Dennis:	Yes, I understand why you'd think that way. Have you heard about due diligence?
Chuck:	No.
Dennis:	This is where an army of attorneys and CPAs in my company check out every nook and cranny of the partnership to make sure that whatever the real estate company promises, they deliver on. This is all done to protect you, Chuck. Now how do you feel about that?
Chuck:	Due diligence, huh?
Dennis:	Is this IRS thing the only part that was of concern to you?
Chuck:	Mostly. Though I guess not anymore. B will you guarantee that this due dilige will forestall any problems?
Dennis:	Can't do that, Chuck . . . But let's l this color chart showing the track re this partnership for the last fifteen ye can see here where it has averaged 3 for seven years straight.

As If technique. He said, "Let's assume it's five years down the road." By using this technique, he found the important points that were motivating Chuck to find a rental house.

7. Dennis played back these three points to check on what he had just heard. This also increased trust and showed Chuck that he cared.

8. Dennis then used a metaphor to get Chuck to identify himself with a successful investor who is sailing in the Caribbean. Dennis used the story to get Chuck to consider a real-estate limited partnership.

9. Chuck produced an objection, which Dennis answered by using psychological sliding. Chuck's objection was visually oriented, so Dennis slid into the kinesthetic mode. He then asked Chuck whether he had any other concerns before he continued. This prevented an objection duel that could have lasted a long time.

10. Then Dennis produced a color graph of the partnership's track record. Chuck's interest skyrocketed because of his need for data that he could look at to comprehend the information better.

11. In concluding, Dennis used a combination of assumptive and choice closes; he assumed that Chuck would buy his proposal, and gave him the choice of when to meet next.

If you value the useful information you've just read, you'll be equally impressed by other products from Nightingale-Conant that focus on career development and personal growth. Learn new techniques for success, such as winning sales techniques, proven customer strategies, and powerful persuasion skills from some of the top authors in the self-development industry.

Nightingale-Conant is the world's leading publisher of personal development audiocassette programs. Our full-color sixty-four-page catalog is filled with innovative and informative programs that teach you how to improve all areas of your life. And with audiotapes, you can learn anytime or anyplace, whether you're in your car, working out, on a plane, or relaxing at home.

Listen to Kerry Johnson speak on this and other important topics. His audio programs available from Nightingale-Conant include:

✔**The Science of Self-Discipline**   6 cassettes   741A
> *Learn how you can gain better control over unwanted habits and accomplish anything.*

✔**Sales Magic**   6 cassettes   512A
> *Master the art of sales by understanding your prospect's subconscious mind.*

To order programs or request a free catalog, call **1-800-525-9000.**
Use the coupon on the book jacket to receive $20 off your order!

Nightingale
Conant
NIGHTINGALE-CONANT CORPORATION
7300 North Lehigh Avenue
Nile, Illinois 60714
1-708-647-0300 • 1-800-323-5552

Chuck: Yes. Wow. That's a lot better than rental property for that time period.

Dennis: One more thing, Chuck. The family sailing in the Caribbean? The reason that they did so well is that they bought into the partnership quickly. If you don't mind, I'm going to call my secretary with the agreement form so we can take advantage of this investment. By the way, shall we meet again next Monday at three or . . . I also have Tuesday at four free.

Chuck: This track record shows that it's exactly what I need. Let's meet again on Tuesday.

How many techniques of unconscious competence did you notice Dennis using? Let's go over them together:

1. Dennis immediately established rapport by talking about Ben Lewis. If you've been referred by someone, *always* mention the person immediately upon meeting.

2. Dennis used humor to relax Chuck. Your clients are as nervous as you are. Even if they groan at your joke, they'll appreciate the effort.

3. Dennis then asked Chuck what financial planning meant to him. This got Chuck to open up a little and talk freely. Use this time to pick out the predicates your client uses. Chuck used visual ones.

4. Dennis complimented Chuck to establish deeper rapport, by saying, "You're obviously familiar with personal economics already."

5. Dennis tried to identify Chuck's outcomes for the meeting by asking what he wanted to accomplish. And he tried to match Chuck's visual mode at the same time.

6. Dennis wanted to get more information on Chuck's outcomes beyond his desire to buy a rental property, so he used the

	have now, but received 28 percent on his invested dollars. He hasn't had to spend even one hour maintaining a rental property. Are you interested in how he did it?
Chuck:	You bet.
Dennis:	He put money into what is called a real estate limited partnership.
Chuck:	Now, wait a second. I've looked at those before. You stick in a pile of money and the IRS may just come along and say, "We don't like this one. It's too abusive." If the company I invest in goes out of business, then I'd be stuck. At least with my own rental house, I know I could write off the losses and improvements.
Dennis:	Yes, I understand why you'd think that way. Have you heard about due diligence?
Chuck:	No.
Dennis:	This is where an army of attorneys and CPAs in my company check out every nook and cranny of the partnership to make sure that whatever the real estate company promises, they deliver on. This is all done to protect you, Chuck. Now how do you feel about that?
Chuck:	Due diligence, huh?
Dennis:	Is this IRS thing the only part that was of concern to you?
Chuck:	Mostly. Though I guess not anymore. But will you guarantee that this due diligence will forestall any problems?
Dennis:	Can't do that, Chuck . . . But let's look at this color chart showing the track record of this partnership for the last fifteen years. You can see here where it has averaged 30 percent for seven years straight.